Roses in the Southern Garden

Roses in the Southern Garden

G. Michael Shoup

Foreword by
Felder Rushing

Published by
The Antique Rose Emporium, Inc.

All text and photographs by G. Michael Shoup
Design by Alison C. Duckworth

Most of the photographs shown in this book were taken in the Antique Rose
Emporium's Display Gardens. Other pictures were taken in private gardens in Georgia,
Louisiana, and South Carolina. Fewer still were from France and New Zealand. Some
photographs and text were taken from previously printed catalogues and reference
guides produced by the Antique Rose Emporium.

Published by the Antique Rose Emporium
9300 Lueckemeyer Rd.
Brenham, TX   77833
www.weAREroses.com

Library of Congress Control Number: 00-102900

Roses in the Southern Garden
G. Michael Shoup
ISBN   0-9678213-0-4
April 2000   Pages XVI, 176   8 1/4 x 10 3/4 hardbound

Printed in the United States of America

Inquiries regarding this book or the Antique Rose Emporium may be
made to 800-441-0002.

To Nicholas

Acknowledgements

One of the great joys of gardening is the commiseration of shared experiences. Over the years of collecting plants and photographs, many people were kind enough to share their gardens with me: Strangers that turned into friends. So it is with gardeners - generous above all else.

I wish to thank Mattie Breedlove, Martha Gonzales, Margaret Sharpe, friends that recently passed away but whose gardening legacy will be remembered. Thanks also to the late Dr. Robert Bayse who showed that the future of the rose looks bright.

Thanks to those who have helped me and the Antique Rose Emporium whether through work, consult or inspiration. Their contribution and encouragement were invaluable. They are in part Stephen Scanniello, Anna Davis, Ruth Knopf, Pam Puryear, Charles Walker, Bill Welch, Joe Woodard, Jim Johnson, Peter Beales, Rick and Donna Emery, Blanche and Wesley Carroll, Carol Kiphart, and George Gray.

I am especially grateful to my co-workers whose hard work and opinions help shape this book: Lynn Smith, not only for your burgeoning creative input but because your worry is enough for everyone. Henry Flowers, for your input seen throughout this book, both in the Antique Rose Emporium Display Gardens design and floral displays. Simon Delgado for gardening with a smile on his face. Betty Schramme and Virginia Tappe who keeps us informed. Rhonda Mainard for her energy. Pat Murphy for his eloquence. Robbie Will and Becky Salinas for their courage. Thank you Glenn Austin for your leadership and the research on Noisettes that is featured in this book. Cindy Ramey for spreading the word in Georgia. Special thanks to Alison Duckworth, this book is largely hers. For the design, the layout and the hours of work, I am indebted. Thanks to Inell Partin for the extra hours of typing so my thoughts could be read. Fran Rogers and Gloria Lehde for their workplace ethic and attitude that make it fun to come to work. Thanks to Terry Tripp and Glenn Schroeter for squaring up the odds in the office. Thanks to Doris Briscoe, Cleo Bimmage, Demetrio Garcia and Alfredo Andrade for staying with me so long.

To Charles Mann for making me a better photographer.

To Julie and Ken Baker, Peter and Cheryl Shoup, and May and Bernie Freeland for not only being family, but living in the right cities.

Thanks to Linda Askey, Melissa Flowers for their critical words and commas. Their help was invaluable and any errors in this book are mine.

Felder Rushing, you say it best!

Mom and Dad, you're great, thanks for the unconditional support.

Lastly and mostly, to Jean, Kelly, Randy and Nick - I love you.

Foreword

I'm reluctant to say this, but it's almost certainly true that you, dear gardener, are not like your neighbors, or you wouldn't have picked up this extraordinary book. Many well-meaning gardeners all around you have decided – after trying for years to do the "right stuff" and failing – that roses are just too hard to grow, and have given up on America's Floral Emblem. Some, like me not that many years ago, have begun bad-mouthing roses. As if tomatoes were easy!

But, at the risk of sounding cynical, don't a lot of romantic ventures begin with what turn out to be more than realistic expectations?

You, however, still have a dollop of hope in your heart, and are willing to risk just a little more precious space in your heart and mind, in your search for romance. This book has been written for you, me, and all others who want much from our gardens, but have many irons in the fire and avoid fussy plants. We garden for love, not challenge.

This book isn't just for us, of course – it's for our neighbors as well, only they don't know it (yet). There's lot's of down-to-earth, practical tips here, of course, along with subliminally seductive photographs. But there's a twist: It's all been gleaned and pulled together by a man who has learned first-hand and through a phalanx of equally-dedicated, knowledgeable Southerners, that not all roses are worthy; he knows that just as some modern roses have been bred to be little more than pretty weenies on bad sticks, some old roses were miserable a century ago and still are.

So between these covers are the absolute best plants for the South, every one put through the rigors of Southern soils, rains, droughts, pests, fickle gardening practices, and all the rest – even outright neglect. They are all survivors, shared or rescued by real gardeners.

If I may get partly personal, if it weren't for Michael Shoup being a down-and-dirty gardener, and such a generous, patient, and supportive man, I wouldn't be growing roses as I do today. He and his peers dusted off my sour attitude, all but forcing me to smell the roses, and proved to me that I don't have to be a dilettante to grow them myself.

I can also attest to Mike the family man, and how he once had to make some hard decisions about his career choice, his ability to earn a living. Roses, he will tell you, saved his life, and to honor them he has been faithful nearly to a fault.

I have accompanied Mike from the dusty back roads of the Texas Hill Country and North Georgia to the cemeteries of Natchez and Charleston. We've loosened our neckties in airports from Chicago to Atlanta, and eaten pecan pie out of our hands while wrestling over the challenges of getting people to give roses another try. And along the way we've examined and discarded some famous roses that simply are not "up to snuff" for Southern gardens.

In my decades of growing roses in the South, visiting and photographing rose gardens and individual rose plants, and even rustling roses by cuttings from old homesites and cemeteries, and after devouring many good books on rose growing, I'm convinced that you are now fondling the very best resource (short of the author himself) you can get your wanna-be-dirty hands on.

These plants, these garden roses, have been a rite of passage for me as a gardener, an act of faith during which I chose to give up some control, get back in the game, and regain my gardening soul. Now I cherish dozens of no-fuss roses of all types, as integral parts of my garden.

Read on, fellow traveler, but don't rest on your petals until you've celebrated these precious plants, their heritage and bounties – by sharing them with your rose-poor neighbors.

Felder Rushing
8th generation Southern gardener

Introduction

As a gardener, I have fallen in love with a gorgeous, seductive, sometimes petulant plant. One that has, along with her beauty, a reputation of being difficult, demanding, aloof, and sometimes plain ornery. Crowned the "Queen of Flowers", she comes with a rich and noble history with bloodlines throughout the ages. She, of course, is the rose, but unlike what Shakespeare said "any other rose would smell as sweet," there exists a dichotomy within roses today that makes them as different as night and day. My love affair is with one side, the forgotten side, of this modern day rose family. My love affair is with the "Antique Rose".

In the last 20 years of growing and selling roses through my company, the Antique Rose Emporium, we have seen my company evolve into one that is now totally committed to the antique rose. The original genestock is still producing the same floral miracles today that were produced centuries ago. During this evolution, we have continued to acquire forgotten and abandoned roses on forays everywhere, as well as receiving cuttings offered from other gardeners. Some have even been acquired from collectors in other lands. The discovery of these found roses and excitement brought about by rose rustling and new acquisitions that were so integral to our formative years has not been replaced but supplemented with a new found love of gardening.

Evaluating, testing, producing and finally marketing these roses required new expansive plots. Land purchased in northern Georgia (Dahlonega) and south central Texas (San Antonio) supplemented our large eight acre spread in southeast Texas (Brenham) as a garden showplace and repository for these plants. Impressions of these roses as they matured became even more profound and awe inspiring. The gardens in Texas and Georgia tested our new foundlings and old varieties in totally different environments. The remarkable ability of Old Garden Roses to perform in such different growing conditions are a tribute to the commanding versatility of these plants. In Brenham (southeast Texas) the rose thrives in flat, open terrain, alkaline soil, 35 inches annual rainfall, and abusive extremes of both heat and cold. San Antonio (south central Texas), hotter and drier, is more punitive than the Brenham location, but still the roses adapt and prosper. In the hilly, forested Georgia terrain, these same roses thrive in acidic soil, heavy clay, and 60 inches annual rainfall. The indigenous flora of the areas and the difference in climate and geography make these three gardens distinctly different and are a testament to the Old Garden Roses' ability to perform in diverse Southern environments.

Those expansive plots of land in Texas and Georgia became more and more creative. Our employees offered new ideas on how old roses could be used. Shrubs, perennials, and vines were added to accent the roses. More fences and ornate structures were built to display them. New themes and styles were explored. The old roses, always hardy and prolific, now through purposeful blending of roses into the landscape, took on a life all its own. We had become passionate gardeners.

I realized that gardening was very personal. Ironically, visits to worldwide botanic rose gardens left me bored. The long perfect rows of the newest varieties were interesting for their color, but something was lacking. Detours into adjacent neighborhoods gave glimpses into individualistic gardens. A window planter filled with colorful perennials and herbs, a small deciduous tree with last year's Christmas ornaments, and potted mums arranged by color were some examples. Occasionally more substantial efforts were seen. Yards with bottle trees and tire planters, small water gardens crowded with horsetail and goldfish, a small border devoted to a color scheme of red or white, fruit trees bordered with parsley, fountains filled with marbles, and ornate vine covered mailboxes were fascinating. There were no rules, only a purposeful decision by someone to mix this with that and see what happened. Even in their simplest form these efforts are fun and of a personal vision. In their more devoted and complex forms they are beautiful and captivating.

We were learning that these roses were different from the modern roses society has become accustomed to, and we wanted everyone to know it. Modern roses are essentially, exhibition roses - short-lived thoroughbreds of erect habit demanding the continuous pampering in order to contribute their overly brilliant perfect flowers. On the other hand, we found that old roses are fragrant and disease resistant, and more importantly, they have a diversity of form that makes them useful as a landscape plant. These roses can embellish the architecture of a fence or home or blend with perennials, annuals, herbs, and shrubs in traditional landscapes. It became apparent that rose breeders, in their efforts to produce perfect long stemmed roses of bright color overlooked these garden qualities that were inherent in the older varieties, whereas the antique roses consistently performed. The proof was in our test plots and display gardens. We had a good product that needed to be brought back into our modern gardens. How could we replace the negative stigmas that were associated with growing traditional roses with these wonderful plants that shared the same name?

Despite the rapid growth of the Antique Rose Emporium and the numerous visitors to our gardens, the message that Old Garden Roses are great garden plants is still relatively unknown to the general gardening public. The uninformed may try Old Garden Roses and plant them in a rectangular rose garden in straight rows like they are accustomed to doing with Hybrid Teas and be perplexed by the resulting wide range of size and form. In their defense, the incredible number of varieties is intimidating. A newcomer to old roses can become frustrated trying to select the right rose for the desired purpose. We've only scratched the surface in our quest to familiarize our customers and ourselves with the proper rose for a particular use. Our work is still ahead of us, but it is made easier once you've seen what we've seen. So with camera in hand, I became determined to show the world that these roses belonged in today's garden. Their inclusion brought beauty and fragrance to our gardens, but even more importantly, I saw the

satisfaction expressed from neighbors and visitors as they languidly strolled through the grounds. It certainly makes the garden a place more grand than the collection of plants that comprise it.

Though our message is the same for both Northern and Southern gardeners, our experience is in the Southern garden. The roses that we've selected for inclusion in this book, in our estimation, are the best possible selections for a variety of uses in the Southern garden. Some would argue that many have been left out, some would even question a few of our inclusions. Nevertheless, the plants selected are ones that we endorse based on years of experience in our Southern gardens.

We have divided our plant profiles into groups based on their best garden use. They are 1) large vigorous climbers (spring bloom and repeat bloom), 2) small mannerly climbers including the cascading Hybrid Musk roses, 3) large shrubs, 4) small shrubs, and 5) specialty plants. In this way the reader can quickly find a plant that would best fit his/her garden need. Each profile will give basic information like date, rose classification, and occasionally some pertinent history, but we've made a concentrated effort to include our experience with growing it, personality, integration into a garden, its fragrance, hardiness, culture, and training.

In conclusion, our gardens are not rose gardens, but gardens that have roses in them. I think the difference is notable. While one can be boring and stagnant, the other integrates roses with a variety of plants (perennials, herbs, annuals, etc.) so that the seasonal evolution of the garden shows the interplay of plants together. Planting roses in association with other plants avoids many of the pests and diseases associated with growing only one type of plant. The diversity increases the stability and performance of the overall garden. You have year-round beauty whether or not the roses are blooming. There is always something creating interest. The garden is an expression created by this mixture. It is infinite and personal.

G. Michael Shoup
Owner, The Antique Rose Emporium

Vigorous Climbers

Once Blooming

Albéric Barbier
Albertine
American Beauty, Cl.
Belle Portugaise
Cherokee
Fortune's Double Yellow
Fortuniana
Lady Banks Roses
Veilchenblau

Repeat Blooming

Céline Forestier
Cecile Brunner, Cl.
Cl. Crimson Glory
Dortmund
Lamarque
Lavender Lassie
Madame Alfred Carrière
Mermaid
New Dawn
Old Blush, Cl.
Reve d'Or

Albéric Barbier, 1900
Rambler

    'Albéric Barbier' has been an outstanding climber for naturalizing and softening the outer perimeter of our garden. Dense canopies of shiny, almost evergreen foliage stretching over fences and arbors were achieved in one year's growth. Plant 'Albéric Barbier' only where it has room to spread and you will soon have birds nesting under its protective cover.

Training vigorous climbers such as 'Alberic Barbier' onto structures such as fences (top), tripods (left) or doorways (right) create entirely different effects. With fences and tripods, roses fill large spaces in the garden and help soften structures with a natural cascade. Doorway roses, more often seen in Europe than the United States, welcome guests with fragrance and color and create a focal point for the house.

Albertine, 1921
Rambler

'Albertine' is one of the most commonly seen ramblers in European gardens. Inclusion in our gardens was a must after seeing the show stopping apricot flowers cover 10 to 20 foot arbors and entryways in their gardens. We have noticed that bloom performance is enhanced when colder winters occur in our Southern gardens. Like rose breeder, Monsieur Barbier's other wichuraianas, 'Albertine's' shiny, dense foliage is one of its finest garden assets and makes for a useful garden addition, even when not in bloom. As with all vigorous climbers, plant to adorn a large structure or fence in a location with lots of sun. Plan to spend time training canes on desired structures to achieve the best results.

'Albertine's' globular flowers contrast with the finer texture of phlox. The gardener also uses monochromatic colors to create harmony in this garden.

'Albertine' (above) is trained casually over an entryway to a children's garden. Here the gardener needs only to drape the vigorously growing canes over the fence and allow them to cascade naturally.

Climbing roses do not attach to structures on their own. The trellis (right) has 'Albertine' canes tied onto the wood lattice. Untidy canes are removed so that all visual emphasis is on the beauty of the flowering trellis.

American Beauty, Cl. 1909
Large Flowered Climber

'Cl. American Beauty' literally stops traffic with its spring bloom wherever we have planted it. This rose, like the previous two profiles, is another wichuraiana hybrid. There was much interest in breeding by using *Rosa wichuraiana* at the turn of the 20th century. Introductions from these crosses resulted in vigorous, glossy foliage and hardy roses, many of them climbers. Many of these new roses had large, fragrant flowers. 'Cl. American Beauty' is often thought to be a sport of 'American Beauty'. It is not. 'American Beauty' was however, one of the parents of 'Cl. American Beauty', and is clearly responsible for the wonderful fragrance and vivid color of this vigorous climber.

'Cl. American Beauty' cascades gracefully off the pillars framing the Southern home in the background. Companions to these roses are peonies, iris and allysum.

'Cl. American Beauty' grows happily with honeysuckle on a picket fence in central Texas. Vigorous roses are complemented with other vines like honeysuckle and clematis.

This sequence of pictures (top, center and bottom) at the Antique Rose Emporium Display Gardens in Georgia shows the maturation of climbing roses on different structures beginning with the appearance of gardens at planting in the first spring, growth throughout the year, and beauty of the following spring.

Arches and a split rail fence provide vertical and horizontal structures to support the vigorous climbers. Rose canes neatly wrapped around pillars, and canes closely attached to the rails of the fence embellish these features. Untrained canes can destroy the harmony of the garden. Walkways serve to divide the beds and give access throughout. Perennials and annuals, including grasses and shrubs, marry with roses within these confines. ('Cl. American Beauty' is planted on the third arch in each picture.)

Belle Portugaise, 1903
Large Flowered Climber

'Belle Portugaise' is the most dramatic rose to drape an arbor in our Southern gardens. Voluptuous, shell-pink flowers hang down like bells on a garland of lengthy canes up to 30 feet. The wild rose from southern China, *R. gigantea*, named for its enormous size and vigor, was crossed with the beautiful Tea, 'Reine Marie Henriette', to sire this romantic 'Belle of Portugal', as it is often called. This rose loves the warmth of our Texas gardens and seems unaffected by its alkaline soil. She is very tender, thriving only in climatic zones 8, 9, 10, thus making her the envy of our Northern neighbors. Occasionally, we have had several years in a row with no blooms due to late freezes, but still consider her a favorite because of her size and romantic beauty. For a gardener anticipating the seasonal changes, 'Belle of Portugal' is a wonderful sight heralding the coming of spring with her very early flush of flowers.

There are many worthwhile climbers that bloom only in spring. 'Belle Portugaise' puts on her annual show with romantic, bell-shaped flowers. It is said that if you can plant but one rose, then plant a rose that blooms throughout the year. But if you can have two roses, make the second choice a once bloomer that puts all its effort into one show-stopping performance each spring.

Cherokee, 1759
R. laevigata
Species

The 'Cherokee Rose' is a native of southern China. It was first botanically described from a specimen growing in Georgia and has been adopted as that state's official flower. Unlikely assumptions have been made that the Cherokee Indians dispersed the plants westward in the Trail of Tears (their forced eviction from their home in Georgia). Thomas Affleck, a prominent Texas nurseryman in the early 1800's, instructed the use of 'Cherokee Rose' as natural hedges. That early use led to its confusion with a more notorious invasive rose, *R. bracteata or* 'Macartney Rose' that had a reputation of destroying farm equipment and strangling cattle. The 'Cherokee Rose' is a vigorous climber up to 30 feet.

With its colorful history, the 'Cherokee Rose' has naturalized throughout the South. Southern gardeners enjoy its graceful habit, dark foliage, and pure white flowers. Unlike many white-flowered plants, you will never see spent brown flowers hanging on like soiled tissue paper. Our gardens feature the 'Cherokee Rose' naturalizing in trees (below), adorning tripods, and cascading on fences. Each form portrays its own graceful personality.

Fortune's Double Yellow, 1845
R. x odorata pseudindica
Species

"Tears come to my eyes when I see 'Fortune's Double Yellow'" says Simon Delgado, a gardener for the Antique Rose Emporium in Brenham, Texas. Upon further clarification, he states, "no other rose can be so beautiful and yet so painful to train." This love-hate sentiment is especially suited to 'Fortune's Double Yellow' for the following reasons: Bright showy flowers are the color of the childhood favorite ice cream treat "Dreamsicles" - peach, cream, yellow and pink all melted together (left), and the canes have prickles that are vicious, not for their size, but for their tenacity of grabbing and inflicting pain. Spilt blood may allow the gardener to bond with certain roses, but not so much as to need a transfusion.

This rose is from southern China and like 'Cherokee' is relegated to our warm Southern gardens where temperatures rarely fall below 15 degrees Fahrenheit. The brightly colored flowers dictate its use as a climbing specimen on fences (below) and enclosed courtyards where the spring bloom temporarily steals your attention from the rest of the garden.

Robert Fortune, 1812 – 1880

Robert Fortune made several journeys to China between 1844-1850. On his first trip, made for the Royal Horticultural Society, he was able to visit Fa-tee Nursery (Flowerland Nursery) in Canton. Through this nursery, plants from China were distributed to the rest of the world via collectors like Robert Fortune, William Kerr, John Parks, and the efforts of the East India Trading Company. The nursery was over 200 years old at the time of his visit. Frustrated at being able to secure plants only through the nursery, he shaved his head save for a pigtail and dressed as a Chinese citizen which allowed him to expand his search. In 1845, while visiting a Mandarin in Mingpo, he found 'Fortune's Double Yellow' and brought it back to England. Other roses he discovered and brought back include *R. fortuniana* and *R. anemoneflora* which are in cultivation today.

The Complete Book of Roses by Gerd Krussmann, Timber Press, 1974

'Fortunes Double Yellow' and 'Fortuniana' naturalize on a fence and enclose the yard around a southern Texas home (left).

'Fortune's Double Yellow' is trained on a Texas kitchen built in the 1850s. The surrounding cottage garden features plants appropriate to the period. Roses are attached to the rock wall using small staples that are inserted into mortar and cracks in the rock. Flexible plant ties and natural jute string is loosely attached to canes and tied to staples so that the attached rose is supported yet not constricted.

Fortuniana, 1845
R. x fortuniana
Species

'Fortuniana' has been used as a root stock for grafted roses because of its ability to thrive in poor, sandy soils. It is resistant to root knot nematode, making it the root stock of choice for Florida gardeners where this pest is a problem. 'Fortuniana' is named after its discoverer, Robert Fortune, a young Scot undergardener who found the rose in Canton, China. *R. fortuniana* is closely related to the Banksias having the same cascading habit and extreme vigor. Flowers are large, white, and very fragrant. We have planted *R. fortuniana* on the southern side of trees where the roses can get full sun while weaving naturally into the trees. Having an oak and rose tapestry burst into bloom in early spring is a memorable sight!

Roses in Trees

Vigorous climbing roses can impart elegance and color in trees of any size in the garden. By planting roses like 'Cherokee', *R. x fortuniana*, and 'Lady Banks' on the south side of an established tree (4 to 6 feet away), canes can be trained and eventually naturalized into the canopy.

Here are some guidelines:

(1) Plant roses only near well established trees that are at least several years old and over 15 feet tall. Deciduous trees are best, including oak, redbud, ash, and elm. Evergreen trees like pine and cedar could also be used.

(2) Plant a rose 4 to 6 feet away from a tree preferably on the south side so they don't have to compete with the tree for sun.

(3) After rose canes reach 8 to 10 feet in length, begin training them on lower and outer branches of the tree. If the tree is tall with few branches, like pines, then it will be necessary to wrap canes around the trunk until they are long enough to reach the lower branches. The following year's canes will naturally weave into supporting branches.

Remember, you want both the rose and the tree to grow and so some judicious prunning will be necessary in future years.

Lady Banks Roses,

Yellow Lady Banks *(R. banksiae lutea)* 1824
White Lady Banks *(R. banksiae alba plena)* 1807
Species

Only 'Mermaid', *R. x fortuniana,* and a few other species can create the massive display that the Banksiae roses are known to achieve. A notable example is the "Tombstone Rose", planted in 1855 in Tombstone, Arizona, which now covers approximately 8,000 square feet (some canes are over 100 feet long). Less notable, but more common, are established plants on abandoned homesites in older neighborhoods that have been allowed to naturalize into trees.

The Banksiae roses can be used many ways in the garden. As untrained cascading mounds they spread to 20 feet and reach heights of 12 feet making freestanding specimens. When covering tripods, they create "houses" - hollow centered structures allowing children to play and hide under veiled canopies. (note: these varieties are thornless.) Wildlife love the refuge offered by these giants. The 'White Lady Banks' is extremely fragrant, and when in bloom, incense of violets permeates through the entire garden.

'White Lady Banks', whose blooms smell of violets, covers a large patio area of this California ranch home.

'Yellow Lady Banks' softens an entryway on an Austin, Texas home.

Banksiae roses are so vigorous that only equally vigorous vines like sweet autumn clematis can grow alongside.

What is the Yellow Rose of Texas?

The yellow rose of Texas was the affectionate name given to the beautiful mulatto woman who was captured by Santa Anna. She not only was able to pass information back to the Texas army, but occupied Santa Anna as well, allowing Texas infantrymen to easily and quickly win the war in a surprise attack. Although this tale is fun and spicy it is not totally satisfying for the gardener determined to find the yellow rose of Texas. Two yellow roses were available to pioneers settling in the Texas wilderness. 'Harrison's Yellow' is well adapted to Northern Texas and has naturalized there. *R. banksiae lutea*, the 'Yellow Lady Banks' rose is well adapted to Southern Texas. A third possibility exists. In late spring a folklorist looking out on a Texas landscape would have seen a sea of yellow flowers on prickly plants. Neither the 'Yellow Lady Banks' nor the 'Harrison's Yellow' rose could have inspired the poet like the brightly colored flowers of the prickly pear cactus.

A Different Point of View

An eye level view of a secret garden entryway shows large shrubs that enclose the garden directing the visitor's view to the statue. Here 'Veilchenblau' gracefully covers an arch emphasizing the statue and defining it as the garden focal point.

An overhead view from the second story of the home shows the beauty of the garden in a more composite sense. The statue, though beautiful, is less significant as the eye is drawn to the colors and patterns of the total garden.

Veilchenblau, 1909
Hybrid Multiflora

The German word 'Veilchenblau' means violet-blue. 'Veilchenblau's' flowers are actually red mauve fading to a bluer hue as they age. Large plants in full bloom can produce thousands of clustered flowers for a stunning display. 'Veilchenblau' is a seedling of *R. multiflora*. Equally as famous but definitely more prone to mildew, is its close relative, 'Seven Sisters'. Other wild forms of *R. multiflora* have naturalized in North America and are considered a pest because of their invasiveness. 'Veilchenblau' is not a pest for us, but a must! It is easy to train, graceful in form, and because of its unique color, wonderful to blend with companions like clematis, honeysuckle, and other flowering climbers.

When left untrained, 'Veilchenblau', (right), will cover small trees and shrubs creating enormous fountains in the landscape. Care should be taken to be sure that the planting stays in the overall scale of the garden.

Céline Forestier, 1858
Noisette

'Céline Forestier' appears to be a small, mannerly climber during the early stages of garden growth. But once established, which may take three to four years, 'Céline Forestier' will achieve substantial size. We've placed her along walkways, on pillars and porches, so that her strong, spicy fragrance can be appreciated. The flat, quartered, pale pink to radiant yellow blooms take on a golden glow in early morning or late afternoon light.

'Céline Forestier' is trained on a pillar in central Texas. Gardener Henry Flowers uses the texture and color of the ornamental grass (pennisetum cultivar Black Moudry) to contrast with and embellish this rose.

Blanche Carroll of Slidell, Louisiana, (below) shows off "Celie's Slidell Pink Tea", an unnamed (found) rose given to her by a neighbor for whom it was named. Blanche said "Celie could root a popsicle stick." "Celie's Slidell Pink Tea" is believed to be a Noisette confirming again the success of this class of roses in the South.

The harvested flowers of 'Céline Forestier', 'Sombreuil' and 'Bouquet d'Or' float in a vase of water creating a dramatic monochromatic arrangement.

Cl. Cecile Brunner, 1894
Polyantha

With tears welling up in her eyes, the elderly lady said, "It takes me back 30 years to when I was on my grandmother's porch." That was her comment as she smelled 'Cl. Cecile Brunner' on an arbor when we first opened our gardens to the public in 1985. This comment is a perfect tribute to the "Sweetheart Rose" as it is commonly known. The fragrance is outstanding and the flowers exquisitely formed. It is no wonder the flower buds are used as boutonnieres and given to loved ones to wear. We hunt for excuses to plant the versatile 'Cl. Cecile Brunner'. The vertical accents soften pillars, fences, and porches while providing stunning flushes of flowers several times a year. Definitely the lady, we often hear her mistakenly called Cecil instead of the feminine version, Cecile.

You can't have your cake and eat it too, is certainly the case as with the florists version of the Red Velvet Cake. Henry Flowers, creative consultant and garden designer for the Antique Rose Emporium, used several hundred 'Cecile Brunner' buds and 'Red Cascade' flowers to make this sweetheart cake.

Only the Nose Knows

The 'Cl. Cecile Brunner' seen on the arbor at left, was planted in 1985. Her fragrance wafts through the garden conjuring remembrances of times past.

Fragrance is the soul of the flower. Roses have many subtle nuances that differentiate them. Distinctions between classes of roses can be determined by their fragrance. Hints of lemon, apple, fruit, wine, damask rose, violets, musk, clove, and nasturtium are all part of the rose fragrance. Many variables affect the presence and intensity of these fragrances - time of day, heat, wind, humidity, and most importantly, the sniffer – him or herself. People are genetically predisposed in their ability to smell. "Noses" for the perfume industry are like tasters for the wine industry and have discriminating senses that can sniff out the smallest of differences.

For the gardener, fragrance of flowers is an important factor in creating a memorable garden. Felder Rushing described this best when addressing an audience. With empty camera and 6-year-old daughter in hand, he would pretend to take a picture of her smelling a rose. He would say, "Now Zoe, put your nose close and take a deep breath, and I will take your picture". He further explained, "One day, thirty years from now, I'll be dead or gone, but she'll come across that rose again and with one sniff, we'll be back together again".

So it is about fragrance . . . .

'Cl. Cecile Brunner' trained on a pillar and arbor provide vertical interest in a perennial bed at the Antique Rose Emporium in Brenham, Texas. Companions of salvia, shasta daisy, and ruellia complete the scene.

Cl. Crimson Glory, 1946
Hybrid Tea

'Cl. Crimson Glory' has cupped, large, velvety red flowers, a rich damask fragrance, and long canes that can be trained. Easily, this makes her the winning choice for our garden. Few modern Hybrid Teas have the qualities to be good garden plants. Bred for their bright colors, strong stems, and exquisite form, they seldom possess the durable qualities that have made older varieties so versatile in the garden. 'Cl. Crimson Glory' is an exception, as it blends perfectly with other plants in the garden. Our gardens feature it on a trellis near our entrance inviting passersby into the garden. Underplanting with pink or white verbenas, petunias, and salvias supplement the festive color.

A pavé of flowers in a wagon features 'Cl. Crimson Glory' (red), 'Belinda's Dream' (pink), 'Sombreuil' (white), 'Graham Thomas' (yellow), and the 'Green rose'.

Prominent colors of red, white, and blue create a festive scene. The cobalt blue pot and benches cool down the garden and calm the viewer. The riot of color offered by the iris, daisies, and the red roses of 'Crimson Glory' energize the viewer adding passion and excitement to the scene. The gardener even color coordinated the clothespins.

Dortmund, 1955
Large Flowered Climber

'Dortmund' is a masculine climber. His large clusters of dark red flowers stand out on vigorous shiny foliage and give stunning accents to pillars, trellises, and fences. The production of hips and flowers together create an interesting contrast. Thorns are mean and numerous, necessitating a training regimen to keep wayward canes from grabbing passersby. 'Dortmund' commands attention as seen by his prolific spring and fall blooms.

'Dortmund' is beautiful whether trained horizontally or vertically. In both cases, careful training ensures proper coverage of the given structure. Excessive canes are removed promoting neatness. The rose 'Ballerina' softens the base of 'Dortmund'.

The menacing face of the gargoyle adds whimsy and folly to this garden. Such well placed features are great focal points in the garden. They also ground the garden, solidifying the scene characterized by the often chaotic plantings that surround them. Here 'Dortmund's' flowers and hips frame the view.

Lamarque, 1830
Noisette

Flowers dripping overhead and spilling out their fragrance are qualities typical of Noisettes. Arbors and entryways covered in Noisettes like 'Lamarque', 'Reve d'Or', and 'Madame Alfred Carriere', when engulfed in flowers, are more beautiful under the trellises and lattice above them. This quality imparts to the garden a Victorian sense of romance and drama unlike traditional climbers that direct their flowers to the sky. Our garden features the fragrant 'Lamarque' roses on a Victorian porch where her canes weave through the white railings. Moonlit nights show her ability to capture light and reflect the feeling that she is the only flower in the garden. As Ethelyn Keays states in her book Old Roses, "the southern moon sheds a lovely light over 'Lamarque.'"

'Lamarque' is not heavily thorned making it an ideal choice for training on porch railings.

'Lamarque' adorns this walkway where her exotic fragrance can be appreciated. Typical of all Noisettes, the blooms face downwards allowing the passersby to enjoy the flowers above their heads.

Old and rotten rafters give way under the weight of 'Lamarque'. Many Teas, Noisettes, and Chinas are proven survivors and can be spotted throughout older neighborhoods in the South.

The garden in winter is reduced in color, texture and form from that of the spring display. It is at these times that other features like symmetry and style can be developed. 'Lamarque's' creamy white flowers gracefully adorn the porch and rails of this Victorian porch in Texas. These vertical accents help frame the sitting area while providing fragrance. Moonlit nights are especially beautiful here, as the dominant white flowers of 'Larmarque' sparkle and reflect the romantic mood.

Lavender Lassie, 1960
Hybrid Musk

"Pink Lassie" isn't as evocative a name as 'Lavender Lassie', but arguably it would be more accurate. We have found the beautiful, medium pink blooms covering a gray wooden wall where they add interest and color. When planted on an archway 'Lavender Lassie' blends perfectly with the Verbena bonariensis and imparts a more formal façade. It is along this walkway that its fragrance can be appreciated. The 15 foot long canes distinguish this rose from most of the other more sturdy Hybrid Musks which are grown as cascading shrubs.

Spiked flowers of foxglove contrast nicely with the 'Lavender Lassie' roses.

Roses and the Company They Keep

Modern roses, bred for showy flowers and often grown for exhibition do not show much tolerance to companion plantings. They are often planted in straight rows like erect soldiers posing for inspection. They all look the same. Old roses have a diversity of forms lends them very well to the garden where underplanting with perennials, annuals, and existing shrubs is desired. Thus the rose is not required to be the sole provider of color, fragrance and form when used in that manner. It becomes just one of a variety of plants in the overall palate that the gardener uses to create his garden masterpiece. In this way, when the roses are in bloom, the garden is beautiful, but even when not in bloom, the garden is beautiful. A diversity of plants in a garden scheme ensures continuity of beauty over time and reduces the burden of any one plant to be perfect at all times.

The concept is having a garden with roses as opposed to having a rose garden.

The herb garden was probably the first such garden to house roses. *R. gallica officinalis*, the 'Apothecary Rose', was a companion to fragrant herbs within the enclosed walls of medieval monastery gardens. Roses, like the herbs, were used for medicinal purposes. Attar of roses, rose water, essence distilled from herbs, were all used to treat ailments of the body. Today's integrated herb gardens are a perfect blend of beauty and function. Herbs can ward off insects and provide contrast of texture and color for the roses.

Cottage gardens and perennial borders, along with theme gardens like a children's garden or a rock garden, all utilize roses with various companions, interpreting the garden to that particular theme. The rhythmic repetition of ornamental grasses and roses in a border, roses embellished with yard art in a children's garden, or native xeriscape plants mixed with wild roses in a rock garden are all examples of different interpretations a gardener may choose.

Madame Alfred Carrière, 1879
Noisette

We consider this to be our most vigorous Noisette, as it sends out dozens of canes that all eagerly reach 20 feet. The nostalgic quality of most Noisettes (exhibiting nodding flowers) is also a great attribute of 'Madame Alfred Carrière'. The canes of this rose are too thick and vigorous for use as a pillar. Accordingly, we've planted her at the base of a Victorian porch so that canes can be trained not only horizontally on rails, but vertically on porch columns. The resulting effect is perfect for the Victorian period from which it evolved.

The famous White Garden in Sissinghurst, England has 'Madame Alfred Carrière' growing on a large 25 foot brick wall. The rose serves as a perfect backdrop to the smaller white flowered shrubs that comprise the garden. Noisettes are tender and can be grown in Zone 6 with only partial success. We have great empathy for Northern gardeners who can't enjoy this rose in their gardens.

Weak flower stems won't support the weight of 'Madame Alfred Carrière's' large blooms. Most Noisette roses exhibit this romantic quality.

'Madame Alfred Carrière' is trained on a brick wall in the White Garden in Sissinghurst at Sissinghurst, England (bottom right). One of the outbuildings at the Governor's Mansion in Austin, Texas (bottom left) is covered with the blooms of 'Madame Alfred Carriere'.

The evolution of a cottage garden in Dahlonega, Georgia is portrayed with the purchase of an I-style building typical of the region (above). The restored building, surrounded by a picket fence, encloses a newly planted cottage garden (right). 'Madame Alfred Carrière' is integrated with mature perennial plantings and contributes to the beauty of this Georgia cottage garden.

Mermaid, 1918
Species Hybrid

    R. bracteata, the 'McCartney Rose', is rampant, extremely thorny, produces suckers and comes up from seeds distributed by birds. As a result, imposing briar patches undaunted by farm equipment has led to its disfavor. 'Mermaid', the result of a cross of this rose and a yellow tea rose, retained the thorniness but does not sucker. It makes a great burglar trap if planted under a window. The drawback is that you will never again want to wash that window.

    'Mermaid' is very popular in England. Jack Harkness, past president of the Royal National Rose Society, gives it his 5 star rating and lists it among the ten finest roses of all time. We have found that it is far more vigorous in the South than is seen in England. This quality along with its vicious thorns has given it a bad name by some gardeners. 'Mermaid' does not belong near streets, doors, sidewalks, or driveways, but should be planted where it can expand without much training. Outbuildings, ugly fences, and neighboring eyesores are great subjects for its magical screening ability.

Careful attention must be given to the placement of 'Mermaid'. Her undaunted vigor and viscious thorns often challenge the gardener's best intentions in training. She is best left to naturalize where training is not necessary. The split rail fence (left) collapsed under her imposing canopy.

The Discovery of Mermaid

In 1976, I started a business growing shrubbery for landscapers in the area. I soon lost interest in the production of the over used exotics and began hunting for native flora that we could offer as alternatives to the repetitious shrubbery that filled our garden centers.

On our forays to hunt native plants, my staff and I also began finding everblooming roses surviving without any apparent care in rather desolate surroundings. This was an enigma to me, for I had never thought of roses as something that could endure the notorious extremes of the Texas climate without a gardener's care. 'Mermaid' opened my eyes. In 1982, while taking an unaccustomed route back to the nursery after a delivery, one of my co-workers chanced upon a huge rose covering a chain-link fence. He made an unauthorized "rustle", brought back flowers and cuttings, and urged me to go see it. It was surviving, indeed, performing spectacularly, in a completely neglected setting, and my first thought was that there must be a landscape niche for such a specimen. A rosarian identified it for me, but I could not find 'Mermaid' anywhere in commerce. Soon, this rose and the other survivors we stumbled across over the next couple of years became the foundation of the Antique Rose Emporium.

It wasn't until 1984 that we discovered that an organized group of Rose Rustlers existed in this part of Texas. (Interestingly enough, they were forming into a loose confederation of enthusiasts just about the time I first saw 'Mermaid'.) Joining the Rustlers opened up a whole world of new varieties. We went out on rustles, swapped "found" roses and talked a great deal about the possibilities of our discoveries.

At the nursery we gave our finds household names like "Old Gay Hill Red China" (for the town where we found it) or "Highway 290 Pink Buttons" (found on Highway 290) to help us remember where we found them. We got help from other rosarians, botanical gardens and literature in our struggle to identify the found roses. Many of them had once been in commerce, in some cases as long ago as 150 years, but only a few remained. Those were our initial criteria: survival and usefulness. Then we realized that old roses are far more wonderful than that. They have a delightful fragrance, are resistant to pests and diseases and exhibit a splendid diversity of forms. Yes, and they flower, too. These roses fit to a "T" the niche I had originally had in mind for Texas native plants.

Note: Although rose rustling would imply stealing or pillaging of plants, it is not. Just a few cuttings should ever be removed from the mother plant, and only after getting permission from the owner.

Spent flowers of
'New Dawn'
gracefully litter the
grass under this
pergola.

The vigorous nature of
'New Dawn' allows for
companions like fast
growing Skyvine
(Thumbergia), to
mingle within this
structure. Such
combinations would
be impossible with
smaller, less vigorous
roses, as they would
be engulfed by such
vines.

New Dawn, 1930
Rambler

'New Dawn' is an everblooming sport of 'Dr. W. Van Fleet'. Sensing great popularity and demand, Somerset Nursery patented this rose in 1930 - the first patent ever to be issued. Their efforts were greatly rewarded as 'New Dawn' is now one of the most recognized names in roses.

'New Dawn' has showy, high-centered, perfectly formed, fragrant flowers. Imagine hundreds of these beautiful flowers on 20 foot canes and you can see why this rose stops traffic. We use 'New Dawn' on fences with clematis or honeysuckle for an informal cascading interpretation, or trained tightly on pergolas and trellises for a more formal design. In both situations 'New Dawn' blooms heavily in the spring, lightly in the summer, and moderately in the fall. We rely upon this rose a great deal as it provides large blooms throughout the season, is cold hardy through zone 5, and can be trained as a climber or cascading shrub.

Cl. Old Blush, date unknown
China

     Some time after 1752, when 'Old Blush', the shrub, was introduced, a climbing form of this plant was discovered. (Climbing sports have naturally occurred from many roses.)

     All the wonderful qualities of 'Old Blush' are available on this vigorous climber. Massive Spring bloom, followed by summer and fall blooms, make this a dependable color accent for any vertical structure. The no-fuss quality of the shrub was inherited by the climber as well.

The Cottage Garden

The cottage garden is one of the most expressive forms of gardening, its uniqueness not only evident from garden to garden, but from year to year. It informally combines plants that have usefulness with plants that are displayed for sheer enjoyment.

The style had its start in England and northern Europe during the renaissance when plant collectors shared their discoveries with the wealthy upper class. Trendy gardens incorporated such new introductions with the vegetables, local wildflowers, and herbs that had always been used. The garden, planted in close proximity to their back and front doors eventually became enclosed by fences, hedges, or walls. Walkways that meander from doorway to gate were composed of rock or gravel, paths that ventured from side to side were of dirt and straw. Walls and fences were plastered with trained and espaliered fruits like grape, peach, and plum. Herbs were nestled close to the door. Lettuce, cabbage and the like were planted in neat rows and flowers littered walkways and front gates with their color and fragrance. Interesting new plants were stuck where they would fit. The resulting artful disarray of practical plants, small trees, and colorful flowers in their unique enclosures became the cottage garden.

Each season brought on new beauty as seen by the placement of newly acquired plants. New combinations were tried along with the gardener's desire to arrange new expressive combinations amongst the other maturing plants.

One of the most enduring plants for the cottage garden has been the rose. The intense fragrance and nostalgic value dictated the passage of roses from one generation to another.

The cottage garden today, with its many international influences, rare plants, and elaborate enclosures and walkways, still basically remains the same as it always has, the expressive garden where the gardener can do anything his fancy desires.

A riot of color, texture, and form is created by the use of old roses, perennials, and annuals in this cottage garden. This 1850's period garden surrounds a restored building at the Antique Rose Emporium (Brenham) and includes 'Cl. Old Blush' on the picket fence, 'Lamarque' trained on the entryway arbor, 'Mutabilis' in the foreground, and 'Souvenir de la Malmaison'.

'Reve d'Or' covers an arbor by the Antique Rose Emporium's office.
Yellow colors and strong fragrance are reminiscent of the 'Maréchal
Niel' roses that popularized the Noisette class in the late 1800's.

'Reve d'Or', shown in the bottom right hand corner of this photo, and
'Jaune Desprez', another notable Noisette rose, are often confused with
each other. Both bloom at similar times with the same fragrance. Since
the colors are changeable depending on the time of year, it is easy to see
why they are often misidentified.

Reve d'Or, 1869
Noisette

'Reve d'Or' occupies several places in our garden. The office arbor and entryway to the Victorian garden are two locations that she has been added. This is a result of succumbing to the "we just have to have more" attitude that one look at this rose will impart. The original planting on the stone wall of an 1850's kitchen looks as if she had been there since the placing of the cornerstone. Training 'Reve d'Or' over the kitchen door allows visitors to look up to the pendulous blossoms as they enter. Noisette roses like 'Reve d'Or' make perfect compliments to southern homesteads which are their birthplace.

Rose blooms will fluctuate in both color and size with temperature changes. Many roses are smaller and less intense in color during the heat of the summer. This variation of color adds interest to the garden. Like all of the Noisettes, 'Reve d'Or' grows in zone 7 or warmer.

II
Mannerly Climbers

Accents   Cascading Hybrid Musks

Accents	Cascading Hybrid Musks
Alister Stella Gray	Ballerina
Altissimo	Buff Beauty
Crépuscule	Cornelia
Jeanne d'Arc	Felicia
Pinkie, Cl.	Kathleen
Sombreuil	Moonlight
Zéphirine Drouhin	Prosperity
	Will Scarlet

Alister Stella Gray, 1894
Noisette

'Alister Stella Gray' is often referred to as the "Golden Rambler" which, in our estimation, is wishful thinking. It's not that it doesn't inspire you with its beauty and healthy growth, but ramble it doesn't. For us, it provides 6 to 8 feet of tidy growth that is considerably smaller than the typical rambler. If the morning or late afternoon sun catches it right, it may look golden. However, for the rest of the day its clusters of yolk yellow buds open into beautiful pompons of creamy yellow that fade to white.

'Alister Stella Gray' makes a perfect, mannerly accent to a rock pillar which reflects the same hues. She is small enough to put into a large pot to accent a patio, door, or mailbox.

At sunrise, 'Alister Stella Gray' glows against the old rock column remains of an entry gate to an historic homestead(right). Accentuated by the early morning light, the gold and cream colors radiate more brilliance.

'Alister Stella Gray' (left) casually covers a 6 foot pillar. A few canes are trained on the post while others cascade in a loose mound around the base and among the perennials .

Altissimo, 1966
Large Flowered Climber

'Altissimo' is so stately that she demands a place of importance in the garden. Her bright red flowers cry out to be used on a showy trellis or accent a grand entryway where her fragrance can also be appreciated. Her regal posture, provided by her stiff canes, portrays a neat and formal quality.

'Altissimo' is useful as a specimen plant and will glady serve as a focal point in any garden.

This formal setting of potted topiaries and the cowardly lion greet visitors at the grand entryway at the Huntington Library in California. The mannerly climber 'Altissimo' adds to the drama of the scene. Training roses to stucco walls without damaging them is important. The façade is preserved by inserting small eye bolts or staples into the wooden eaves and trim around the windows. Wire is then stretched through the eye bolts or staples creating a lattice for support.

Crépuscule, 1904
Noisette

The Noisette roses are recognized as the first rose class originating in the United States. Their history reads like a modern day soap opera complete with mistresses, greed, and power (see below).

Crépuscule was introduced rather late compared to most other Noisettes. The earlier Noisette varieties tended to have small flowers, while the later rose introductions had larger flowers resulting from crosses with larger flowered Tea roses. Crépuscule is an example of the latter, offering 3 inch fragrant flowers that repeat beautifully in the fall. We have grown her framing a kitchen window on a restored 1800s Victorian house where her mannerly canes reach 10 feet. Here the sight and fragrance of her can be enjoyed not only from the garden, but from inside the house as well. Whether grown on walls, fences, arbors, or pillars, Crépuscule is indispensible where a period effect is desired, especially in the South where the Noisettes originated.

Noisette Roses
The American Rose

The history of the Noisette Roses is a tapestry of human events and achievements; a record of triumph and entrepreneurial spirit woven into the fabric of a changing genteel society. It blends the pleasures and pursuits of gardening with the fortunes of men.

We begin in 1802 at "The Garden," an appropriately named rice plantation just outside of Charleston, South Carolina with the owner, John Champneys and neighbor, Philippe Noisette. Mr. Champneys was in possession of a rose of great distinction, *R. moschata*. With this rose and 'Parson's Pink China', a new class of roses would emerge. A seedling of *R. moschata* with 'Parson's Pink China' as the pollen parent was raised by Mr. Champneys, and called *R. moschata hybrida*. This event alone makes this a noteworthy rose, and it was viewed by many as "the first true hybrid rose". While this claim may not be strictly true (Gregor Mendel would not formulate the rules of heredity until 1866) this was without doubt the first hybrid rose with repeat bloom. That, along with its graceful form, fragrance, and ease of care led to its rapid increase in popularity.

John Champneys presented two tubs of six

plants each to William Prince of New York from which "an immense number were propagated and sent to England and France". Champneys had already given the rose to Philippe Noisette, who had begun to market it in 1811 as 'Champneys' Pink Cluster'. From seedlings of 'Champneys' Pink Cluster' Philippe raised another promising rose which he called 'Blush Noisette'. In 1817 he sent both plants and seeds to his brother Louis in Paris. Louis named the best of these seedlings 'Rosier de Philippe Noisette' after his brother, and the remainder, although named, became known as simply 'Noisette Roses'. They became so exceedingly popular that 'Rosier de Philippe Noisette' was painted by Redoute just three years after its French debut.

John Fraisier, also of Charleston, repeated Champneys crosses and in 1818 produced 'Fraisier's Pink Musk' which he carried to England. It seems that Mr. Fraisier, as well as others, endeavored to have this viewed as another class, the Musk Class of Roses, but they became quickly aligned with the Noisettes.

The popularity of the Noisettes stems from their fresh and unique traits. First of all, the roses bloomed in huge panicles, bearing as many as 70 individual flowers in each cluster. Additionally, there is the truly graceful habit of these roses which allows them to be used in many different garden settings, but especially as climbers, or more appropriately as pillar roses. It was this same grace that led to its distribution throughout the genteel southern states.

Seedlings of 'Champneys' Pink Cluster', and the Noisettes' roses continued to charm rosarians, and additional crosses were tried. Thus it was, that in 1830 the first "vigorous" yellow rose, 'Jaune Desprez', was produced. Exact parentage is unclear, but the general view is that either 'Blush Noisette' or 'Champneys' Pink Cluster' was crossed with 'Parks' Yellow Tea Scented China'. The resultant offspring was a vigorous climber to about 20 feet with peach shaded yellow flowers frequently edged with pink. The flowers were also much larger than previous

noisettes had shown, and as a result further crosses of Noisettes with Tea roses became the order of the day. The Tea blood gave larger size to the blooms, but also reduced their number, as well as adversely affecting the ability of these new roses to withstand severe cold. However, for rose growers in the American South, the Noisettes were ideal.

Noisettes in general form large vines which are well suited for training on pergolas, arbors, or walls. They are frequently well displayed on pillars, or the large columns of stately manors. The clusters of roses repeat magnificently in the autumn. Fragrance varies with the variety, but is strong and usually sweet. Color of the flowers are generally pastel blends, with shades of white, pink, or yellow dominating. There are some that are nearly red, but they are the exceptions.

'Champneys' Pink Cluster' is usually grown as a free standing shrub or short climber. As a shrub, the long slender canes reach upward to about six feet, and then bow gracefully under their burden of buds and blooms, creating a lovely effect; much as if some giant had stuck his ladylove's bouquet in the garden for safe keeping. When grown as a short climber, 'Champneys' Pink Cluster' is best displayed on a fence or trellis. In this way the supple canes can be fanned out, or espaliered, inviting a closer approach by the appreciative observer. At times the semi-double blooms can be almost solid, covering the entire breadth of the plant.

For settings requiring larger climbers, there are a multitude to choose from. 'Jaune Desprez' and 'Lamarque' are both vigorous and can easily cover an arbor or pergola. Their canes are quite flexible, and hence lie down well on an overhead structure. When grown in this way, the soft cream flowers of the 'Lamarque' or the brighter apricot hues of the 'Jaune Desprez' blooms peer down at one, as if they were trying to judge the reaction their lovely perfume has had on those passing below. On a pillar or column, the golden tones of the semi-double 'Reve d'Or', or the rich yellow of the full, almost quartered 'Celine Forestier', blooms are shown to great advantage. The stiffer canes need to be trained around the support, or fanned out laterally to encourage flowering all along their length. For colors more pink than those just mentioned, look to the large blooms of 'Madame Alfred Carrière'. Though quite pale, and frequently perceived as white from a distance, these fragrant, double flowers, are typical of the pink colors of the Noisettes. The new buds of rich pink quickly cool to a soft cameo white, as if embarrassed at first being seen, but regaining their composure with maturity. 'Madame Alfred Carrière' should only be grown on a tall wall, or into a sturdy tree, as the canes are quite stiff and grow incessantly toward the heavens.

Perhaps the purest white of the Noisettes is to be found in the semi-double blooms of 'Jeanne d'Arc'. Quite mannerly in habit this rose is used to best advantage as decoration for a low fence or small out-building. Spreading the canes not only grants more space for the profuse clusters of blooms, but also allows the bright red hips to be readily observed. Philippe's 'Blush Noisette' should be grown in a similar manner, although it shows well as a free standing shrub.

While the passage of time has moved the south into a different era, these roses can evoke the nostalgia of bygone times. They are still encountered at many homesites and cemeteries, and are being re-introduced by appreciative gardeners and historians. 'Champneys' Pink Cluster' was recently proclaimed the "official rose of the City of Charleston", and it has a position of honor in Charleston's Noisette Memorial Garden. John Champneys and Philippe Noisette may no longer be with us, but the gift of beauty and fragrance they gave us has made them part of the present as well as the past.

Flowers cascading from a trellis add a touch of romance to the Southern garden, a role easily performed by Noisette roses, in this case, 'Crépuscule'.

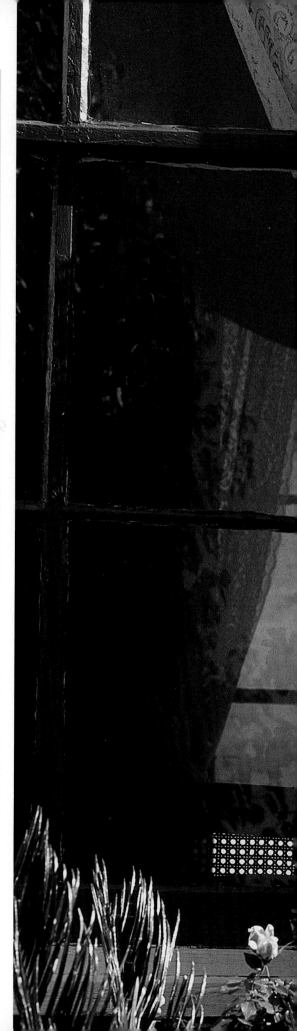

Jeanne d'Arc, 1848
Noisette

'Jeanne d'Arc' is one of few small, mannerly climbers in the Noisette class of roses. Truly a Southern aristocrat in its breeding and style, it is perfect for conveying the impression of a mid-1800s Southern garden. Noisettes have the ability to create vertical accents that are unique among roses, producing flowers that hang from their supports. 'Jeanne d'Arc' is an ideal pillar rose to 7 feet or cascading shrub that mounds to 4 feet. Like all Noisettes, it betrays its Musk ancestry by a grand fall display and strong fragrance. Small red hips, the size of peas, often appear at the same time as the flowers in the fall making for a unique color contrast with the white flowers.

The pristine, clean white flowers of 'Jeanne d'Arc' are reflective of the chapel's purity. The linear textures from the inflorescence of ornamental grasses, Muhlenbergia capillaris *and* Miscanthus transmorrisonensis *give interesting contrast to the flowers.*

Cl. Pinkie, 1952
Polyantha

'Cl. Pinkie' is the single most versatile rose a garden can have. The gardener has so many choices when using this rose. 'Cl. Pinkie' does it all! She cooperates so willingly that we have used her as a free standing shrub, cascading informally in rows as a hedge, adorning the pillars of a gazebo, and trained formally on trellises. She even provides an elegant touch to large pots when allowed to cascade over the sides of the container. In all cases, companions like herbs, perennials, annuals, or shrubs blend perfectly with her. 'Cl. Pinkie's' clusters of fragrant, pink flowers bloom repeatedly through the temperate months, April through October. The nearly thornless quality of this rose makes it a joy to train. 'Cl. Pinkie' is hardy enough to extend to zone 5 but is happiest in the South.

*The style and
personality of the
garden is limitless
when using versatile
roses like 'Cl. Pinkie'.
A gardener can
create dramatic
pillars or cascading
drifts to create
continuity. By
planting on a rustic
fence, 'Cl. Pinkie'
defines and accents a
cottage garden.*

*Viewing the same garden bench from opposite sides shows the
strength of line in the garden. From one side the eye is led by a drift
of 'Cl. Pinkie' roses to the house and cottage garden, and from the
other, into the hills and forest.*

Sombreuil, 1850
Tea

Stephen Scaniello and Tanya Bayard point out in their book <u>Climbing Roses</u>, that there is much confusion regarding the 'Sombreuil' of today and that which was described and illustrated in earlier literature. Qualities such as increased cold hardiness (zone 5), mildew resistance, unique fragrance, and globular buds are distinctions which are not common to Tea roses but are evident in this rose. Whether it is or isn't the original 'Sombreuil', today's version is beautiful in our gardens. Stiff canes to 12 feet behave obediently as they fan out on trellises. Pillars and small fences can support the glossy leafed canes and work as a perfect backdrop to the delicate flowers. Creamy white petals, imbricated like the feathers on a dove's neck, swirl within the saucer sized flowers.

'Sombreuil' graces an old picket fence at the Antique Rose Emporium's gardens in northern Georgia. Foxglove and clematis grow nearby and add interest and color to the cottage garden.

Zéphirine Drouhin, 1868
Bourbon

Bright, cerise pink flowers, fragrance, and cold hardiness (zone 5) are among 'Zéphirine Drouhin's' many assets. However, these may not be 'Zéphirine Drouhin's' best quality. Thornlessness is. We readily use her in areas of high traffic, such as on arches, along pathways and in our children's garden. Canes are flexible and easy to train on pillars, arbors and trellises. In all cases, full sun is best even though 'Zéphirine Drouhin' has been erroneously touted as doing well in the shade.

'Zéphirine Drouhin' on an arbor in a cottage garden in early spring (left) and late spring (below).

The Trained Climber

One of the worst distractions to an otherwise beautiful garden is the visual chaos created by an improperly trained climbing rose. In some gardens, climbing roses can casually weep from fences or mound over themselves making wonderful additions without the hours of laborious training. Many gardens though, employ the use of arches, pillars, pergolas (covered allées) and trellises. These structural forms, along with the outside walls of homes, are beautiful architectural features that demand tasteful ornamentation worthy of their cost and stature.

As gardeners we must harness the rose and not let the rose harness us. Canes of climbing roses must be tightly woven around these structures. Excessive canes or canes that can't be trained should be removed. In this way, the structure is embellished and beautified by the rose. Trellises can be made out of metal or wood and in themselves can be very ornate. A good construction size for trellises, large enough to support climbers, is from 8 to 12 feet tall by 4 feet or larger in width. Most ready-made trellises are too small and weak to support a climbing rose. Training the rose horizontally through the weave offered by trellises not only keeps the rose tidy looking, but increases its bloom as well. Pillars and arches create very dramatic transitions and specimens in the garden. Flexible caned roses like 'Zéphirine Drouhin' are ideal for archways where a softer effect is desired. This is also very effective in a series of arches creating pergolas.

'Zéphirine Drouhin' on a pillar during winter shows canes wildly growing in every direction. Older canes should be removed, thinning out the plant in favor of the younger, more vigorous canes. These remaining canes are trained spirally around the post to increase the bloom performance and tidiness of the pillar.

59

Ballerina, 1937
Hybrid Musk

'Ballerina' is an outstanding landscape plant with qualities typical of the Hybrid Musks. Although it was introduced years after the death of Rev. Joseph Pemberton, it is still thought to be a result of one of his crosses. Pemberton, 1850–1926, was instrumental not only in introducing many of the Hybrid Musk roses, but also re-establishing the rose as England's national flower and creating The Royal National Rose Society, as it is known today. By crossing some of the early Hybrid Teas and Polyanthas with a form of *R. moschata* he produced many wonderful Hybrid Musk roses. 'Ballerina' produces a dense canopy of leaves on a spreading bush of 4 feet. Hardy and carefree with a hint of fragrance, it lends itself especially well to mass plantings or for formal hedges. The flowers are small but occur in large heads throughout the spring and fall, fall bloom being more spectacular than spring. We've not only used it along a parking lot softening the noise and improving the view to our gardens, but also among yellow flow-ered perennials in an enclosed cottage garden.

Ballerina bursts into spring bloom in this garden in Atlanta. Clusters of flowers, informal cascading habit, and a good fall bloom make it a wonderful plant for the Southern garden.

The Hybrid Musk Roses

The Hybrid Musks were originated by Peter Lambert in 1904 but perfected by the Englishman, Rev. Joseph Pemberton. Although the Hybrid Musks owe more of their parentage to 'Trier' than to the Musk Rose, they are nevertheless called Musks because the musk scent was detectable in the earliest varieties. Pemberton crossed Trier with Teas, Hybrid Teas, Chinas, and Hybrid Perpetuals to produce this versatile class of roses. Introductions like 'Cornelia', 'Felicia', and 'Moonlight' are shrubs that grow like graceful cascading fountains, enabling the gardener to use them as either climbers or as a free standing shrubs. Other introductions included roses like 'Penelope' and 'Bishop Darlington' that exhibited a more upright habit of growth.

Flowers occur in spring but can be more impressive in the fall, especially in the South where plants grow very large through the summer. The clusters of flowers are beautiful pastels and blends, the fragrance is outstanding, and the foliage is handsome and disease resistant. Because of the loose open, habit of growth, they have successfully been used in partial shade without sacrificing their graceful appearance. However, the number and quality of flowers are decreased in the shade. A sunny exposure is preferable with all roses. In the Rose Annual for 1968, Graham Stuart Thomas summed up the Hybrid Musks: "Unless some keen spirit is prepared to produce some richly colored shrub rose along the lines adopted by Pemberton, I think this group should remain as it is: carefree flowering shrubs of the greatest value for our gardens at mid summer or later, delightfully fragrant, and in a fair range of colors, and superb value for hedging." Considered as such, Joseph Pemberton served us well.

Buff Beauty, 1939
Hybrid Musk

Though slow to establish in its first year, 'Buff Beauty' is well worth waiting for in later years for its color and floriferousness. Flowers are apricot-orange in early to mid Spring when night temperatures dip into the 40's and 50's. Later flushes of flowers in the warmer late Spring and early Fall are muted to a creamy apricot color. The habit of this rose is more sinuous and feminine than that of the other chunky Hybrid Musks. 'Buff Beauty' will grace a pillar or entryway or loosely cascade over itself if left untrained as a free standing shrub. Although it performs well in shadier spots of the garden, thicker growth and more blooms will be evident in the sunnier areas of the garden.

'Buff Beauty' is one of the taller Hybrid Musks. When trained on a pillar near a walkway, passersby enjoy her elegance. Fallen petals add to the charm of this garden.

A sturdy, rustic arbor (right) provides the necessary support for 'Buff Beauty' in this Georgia garden.

Cornelia, 1925
Hybrid Musk

'Cornelia' is a rose that gets bigger and better each year. It is not uncommon to have a plant 6 feet tall and 8 feet wide forming a fountain of coral pink flowers in both spring and fall. Because of her size and the unusual strawberry-pink flowers with a musky fragrance, we planted her near a walkway around our water garden. 'Cornelia' is hardy in zone 6 and warmer.

'Cornelia's' placement at water's edge (above) in this rock garden allows her graceful arching form to blend perfectly with Louisiana iris, verbenas, and grasses. Old garden roses have a diversity of form that allows them to mix with many different garden styles and themes. Hybrid Musks like 'Cornelia' can go on for several years before pruning or thinning is necessary then taking out older, less productive canes in favor of the younger ones is all that is required. This type of thinning maintains the natural graceful habit of this rose. If the plant has grown bigger than appropriate to the garden, then reducing the entire plant by 1/2 to 1/3 prior to the onset of growth in the spring will bring it back into scale. Roses cut back in this way explode with foliage and flower usually within a few months of such drastic measures. Many roses, like Hybrid Musks, that repeat their bloom, usually improve in the quality and quantity of bloom when this method is employed.

Hybrid Musks are versatile and can be trained as climbers or left free standing as shown in these two gardens. A fountain of flowers is created by 'Cornelia' (above). 'Trier', the parent to many of the Hybrid Musks shares the arbor with 'Will Scarlet' in the background. The tripod (right) at the Antique Rose Emporium in Georgia is trained with 'Cornelia', as a climber.

Felicia, 1928
Hybrid Musk

'Felicia' is a very graceful rose. In our garden we have her weeping over a rock wall in the herb garden where her fragrance, which is the most intense of the class, can mingle with all the other aromas. Her dainty quality sets her apart from the other rotund Hybrid Musks that Joseph Pemberton produced. We reward ourselves with as much of her presence that space allows. Whether planted in large containers, featured on garden structures, or used in arrangements, she is a gardener's dream. 'Felicia' is cold hardy to zone 6 and warmer.

Grown on the water well in the upper left portion of this photo, 'Felicia' competes with the colorful vegetables, annuals, and vines in Mr. McGregor's garden, a childrens garden at the Antique Rose Emporium.

'Felicia' spills over the rock wall of this herb garden in Texas. Roses, like most herbs, are edible and make colorful additions to salads and decorations to cakes.

Kathleen, 1922
Hybrid Musk

The simplicity of the single white flowers of 'Kathleen' compliment the graceful form of this bush. Small flowers borne in large clusters on arching canes over shade loving perennials like hostas and ferns make for a pleasing combination.

'Kathleen' can tolerate some shade, but the number of flowers and the density of the plant will suffer. Hybrid Musks in general have a shape and form that lend them to the shadier spots of the garden. The open, graceful cascading branches that characterize them is actually embellished with less sun.

'Kathleen's' white flowers define her spreading form. The dense foliage of this rose provides good cover for birds which are often found nesting in well-established plants.

Moonlight, 1913
Hybrid Musk

We have made the unfortunate discovery that white roses are not "en vogue". Ironically, white-flowered roses are very dramatic and inspirational when used properly in a garden setting. 'Moonlight' is a large cascading shrub that can be easily trained on a pillar, trellis, or small arbor. The reflective quality of the white flowers is stunning when backed by the dark foliage of other large trees and shrubs. In these situations her flowers glow - outlining the natural grace and beauty of her form. The rose 'Moonlight' is especially captivating on moonlit nights.

'Moonlight' begins to climb on a tripod in the Antique Rose Emporium gardens in Georgia. The tall trees provide a dark background which makes white roses stand out.

Prosperity, 1919
Hybrid Musk

'Prosperity', another white-flowered Hybrid Musk, has captured the admiration of many of our gardening friends. Shiny, dark green foliage provides contrast to the large clusters of white flowers. Perfect for a pillar rose, 'Prosperity's' canes are stiffer than average for a Hybrid Musk, making it the plant of choice for a number of highly visible posts and arbors in our gardens. Fragrance is delicate like its Tea parent, 'Perle des Jardins'. Like the other Hybrid Musks, it is also hardy into zone 6 making it widely adaptable throughout the South and East.

'Prosperity's' bright white flowers create the larger than life illusion in this Southern garden(right). At sunset this illusion is even more dramatic capturing and reflecting light.

Bordered walkways edged in herbaceous plants are layered in various textures, forms, and colors. Such gardens usually have smaller, creeping plants near the walkway with taller, upright shrubs and grasses behind. This method of planting frames all the plants for the best view from the walkway. Repetition of certain color and form give rhythm and balance to the garden, helping to tie the mixtures together. 'Prosperity', hardly visible in this picture(left), provides a vertical display at the end of the walkway ending behind the bird houses. Trained climbing roses behind mixed borders give added dimension to these gardens which are usually backded by stout, non-flowering shrubs.

Will Scarlet, 1948
Hybrid Musk

Left as a free-standing shrub, 'Will Scarlet' will be as wide as he is tall. This wouldn't be so remarkable except that these dimensions can reach an 8 feet by 8 feet. We have also used him as a climber on a pillar. His flowering habit produces a fine spring display which is followed by an equally spectacular show in the fall, leaving clusters of round orange hips. 'Will Scarlet', like many of the Hybrid Musks, needs little if any pruning. The naturally arching form simply covers up prior years growth so that the plant literally gets bigger and better year after year.

The large pot anchors this garden scene, stabilizing the view from all the color and texture in the surrounding plantings.

'Will Scarlet' produces a respectable display of red flowers even in this partially shaded garden. Hybrid Musks have been touted to grow in light shade, but more sun exposure will always create more flowers.

III
Large Shrubs

Chinas

Archduke Charles
Cramoisi Supérieur
Louis Philippe
Mutabilis
Old Blush

Teas

Baronne Henriette de Snoy
Bon Silène
Duchesse de Brabant
Madame Antoine Mari
Marie van Houtte
Mrs. Dudley Cross
Monsieur Tillier
Safrano

Other Shrubs

Belinda's Dream
Graham Thomas™
Heritage™
Katy Road Pink
Lafter
Maggie
Marchessa Bocella
Penelope
Puerto Rico
Souvenir de la Malmaison

Archduke Charles,
Prior to 1837
China

We are so lucky to have at our beckened call a rose like 'Archduke Charles'. Imagine a plant that blooms with fragrant flowers of red, pink, and white, blooms repeatedly March to November, and doesn't mind being planted with colorful companions like perennials and annuals. One of the showiest China roses, 'Archduke Charles' does all these things without becoming a maintenance burden. Shear just once or twice a year to keep it full and of appropriate size to the garden. Our 1850s restored stone kitchen has 'Archduke Charles' planted as a foundation hedge so that we can admire him not only from afar, but from the porch above. Plants are tender, so plant in zone 7 or warmer.

'Archduke Charles' with its long flowering season is planted as a colorful hedge to soften and beautify this rustic building (left). Adding color and diversifing the plantings gives style to this form of landscaping.

This sequence shows changes in the seasonal beauty of 'Archduke Charles' and perennials on the south side of an 1850 restored building at the Antique Rose Emporium. Roses are kept below the porch by shearing them in early spring and early fall. This keeps plants at their best kept size of 3 to 4 feet while not overpowering the scale of the garden. Mulches are added in the winter and summer around roses and perennials. This carefree garden is shown during the winter (above), spring (middle), and fall (bottom).

Mustache landscapes, like shown above, are very common. They are typified by the solid green hedge planted in front of and curving around the home's foundation like the hair on a man's face.

Cramoisi Supérieur(Agrippina), 1832
China

This plant and the rose 'Louis Philippe' have often been mistaken for each other. 'Cramoisi Supérieur' flowers are cupped, rich crimson color with a silvery reverse differing from 'Louis Philippe' in the absence of the white streaking near the base of the flower. (Both plants at certain times of the year can produce mimicking flowers.) 'Cramoisi Supérieur' is excellent as a shrub or to plant at the back of the flower border, or in a large pot. Gertrude Jekyl, in a very British manner, pronounced it, "Capital!" and for us it certainly is. 'Cramoisi Supérieur' is one of the old roses that can still be found in the country gardens of Texas and the South, often handed down from one generation to the next.

'Cramoisi Superieur' survives throughout the South in many old neighborhoods. Carefree plants can attain a size of 6 feet, but the rose looks best if maintained at 4 to 5 feet.

Louis Philippe, 1834
China

One of the first Texas plantings of 'Louis Philippe' was at Lynchberg, Texas, home of Lorenzo de Zavalla, Texan's minister to France in 1834 who brought this and other roses back with him from the Court of St. Cloud. Unfortunately his house site and cemetery are now swallowed by the industries along the Houston ship channel. Round, cup-shaped flowers of 'Louis Philippe' are rose crimson with streaks of white adorning healthy-foliaged shrubs. These carefree, chunky shrubs still survive in cemeteries and at abandoned homesites where care from human hands has ceased many years ago. Unfortunately, this rose is tender, growing in zones 6 and higher. Northern gardeners cannot enjoy these plants whose constant bloom and fragrance make them one of China's greatest gifts to man.

My Rose Rustling Friend

Mrs. Carl Meyer graciously poses for a picture, showing her rose, 'Louis Philippe', which was passed down to her from her mother. Such time-tested heirlooms are abundant in her garden. She helped re-establish lost and forgotten plants by generously sharing cuttings with nurseries like the Antique Rose Emporium. For years she rooted passalong plants in paper cups and clay pots making visits to her garden like going to a mini arboretum of time-tested plants. Gardening the way of her mother and her mother's mother, Mrs. Meyer is a wonderful living example of our gardening heritage.

Mutabilis,
Prior to 1894
China

    'Old Blush' and *R. chinensisx* 'Mutabilis' are great examples of China roses whose flowers tend to darken with age as opposed to other roses that fade. Single petals open yellow-orange, changing to pink and finally falling off the bush as crimson red. "The Butterfly Rose", named because these multi-colored flowers appear to be butterflies clustering on the foliage, is undoubtedly the most sought after rose in the garden. Robust shrubs 6 feet tall and wide are perfect specimens for blending with annuals or perennials of any color. Bronze new growth in early spring expands further the colors offered from this interesting rose. Plant only where temperatures never fall below 10 degress Fahrenheit.

'Mutabilis' livens up gardens throughout the South. Flowers appearing like multi-colored butterflies perch on the foliage in a Georgia rose garden.

We're Talking About Hue!

Color is but one of several important aspects of garden design. Structure, form, and scale are often taken for granted but they are more important to the foundation of a good garden design. However, color is often the most dramatic part of the garden, especially when plants are in peak bloom. Green tends to harmonize with other colors and gives a sense of balance to the garden. Gardens are predominantly green throughout the year, giving the viewer a sense of peace. Orange and yellow are stimulating colors. Gardens incorporating these colors are cheerful and bright creating an illusion of space. They are best used when positioned in front of dark foliaged plants. Red hues are exciting and energizing. Red is a passionate color, representing love and anger. It can also create a festive mood. Blue colors are cool and relaxing. Their hues in a garden will unify and enhance its size. Pink is a blending color embellishing other colors. White is pure, divine, and clean. Very reflective, white is beautiful on moonlit nights and during early evening strolls through the garden. Mixing colors can be tricky, but combinations are often more dramatic than if used singly. Yellow/purple, orange/blue, red/green, all opposites on the color wheel, making for striking contrasts when used together.

Old Blush, 1752
China

Thought to be one of the four stud roses (roses that have been instrumental in modern breeding), 'Old Blush' dominates the field when selecting for outstanding traits in a rose. Grown for well over 200 years, it has passed its incredible blooming prowess to countless cultivars during the history of hybridization. 'Old Blush', with clusters of pink flowers fading to red blooms constantly with heavier flushes occurring during spring and fall. The flowers have a subtle fragrance and the foliage is neat and healthy, thereby making these plants useful as hedges, specimens, or even large pot plants. Our hedge is not allowed to get over 5 feet tall which requires two shearings a year. We prune before the onset of new growth in spring and again in fall. This reduction rewards us with a threefold increase of flowers on a more compact bush. 'Old Blush' has, like all Chinas, a much greater tolerance to alkaline soils, as proven by survivors growing throughout the Texas Hill Country. Gardeners fuss over her beauty, but not her care.

If you have but one plant, let it be 'Old Blush'. 'Old Blush' is the entire landscape of this modest home in Texas.

Creating Your Paradise

There are many different faces to a garden. Gardens reflect the personality of the gardener. Plants chosen can be one monochromatic color, of one genus of plants. They can be expressions of whimsy and folly or themes like herb, water, and shade. They can be informal or formal, enclosed or open. They can be as small as an old boot or of unlimited size. Often times the gardener is intimidated and strangled by too many rules. But the passionate gardener learns by doing. There is no right or wrong, only an evolution of change based on preference and experience. Gardens have become the dynamic expression of the gardener. These are the gardens, simple or complex, that capture the imagination of the visitor. They are personal and infinite.

The garden in late winter (left) before spring's colorful explosion. The same primitive willow twig chair becomes a beckoning focal point in this cottage garden. 'Old Blush' acts as a colorful neighbor to the left. Hollyhocks, dianthus, larkspur, iris, and gladiolus share in this repose.

Baronne Henriette de Snoy, 1897
Tea

'Baronne Henriette de Snoy' is a magnificent Tea rose. The large bush bears beautiful quartered flowers of pastel pink. Stunning displays of over 100 flowers are not unusual for this massive plant. Fragrant old Tea roses like 'Baronne Henriette de Snoy' are commonly referred to as Grandma's roses. Left alone except for some minor pruning, this plant can attain a height and spread of 8 feet. Slightly hardier than most Teas, this rose can be planted in zone 6 or warmer.

'Baronne Henriette de Snoy' and other old Teas fill this table with color, fragrance and memories. Tea roses are as useful today as in the past - fragrant, carefree, and long-lived.

'Baronne Henriette de Snoy' still survives in older Southern neighborhoods where it can easily grow to 8 feet with equal spread.

Bon Silène,
Prior to 1837
Tea

'Bon Silène' represents one of the oldest varieties in the Tea class. Typical of the class, 'Bon Silène' blooms throughout the growing season which can be March to November in some parts of the South. Flowers emerge from deep rose-colored buds and develop into medium pink flowers. Fragrance is cool and distinctive, somewhat like the tea that we drink. We take this solid performer, for granted, placing her anywhere color is needed.

Cuttings are taken on mature, well-labeled plants at the Huntington Botanic Garden in California (below). These gardens are great repositories of rare and endangered roses. With special permission, growers are allowed to propagate these roses for distribution.

Making the Cut

Fall has proven to be the best time to take cuttings in the South, although we have had moderate success with late spring cuttings. During the heat of the summer, most roses do not tend to grow actively, however they do rebound in the fall. Once the new growth has stiffened, we select a pencil-thick stem as our cutting. (Growth that is too new has soft tissue that will wilt quickly once cut.) Cut the

stem into lengths containing 2 to 3 leaflets each (see photo at left). The bottom cut should be just below a bud eye. The cuttings are stuck in a well drained potting soil (a styrofoam coffee cup with a pierced bottom works well as a pot). Place a plastic bag over the top as a canopy (supported by straws to keep it off the cuttings). Place in a warm area with lots of humidity and indirect sunlight. High humidity can be accomplished by misting periodically during the day for the first two weeks (a spray bottle works fine). Your rose should root within three to six weeks, but some varieties are difficult, so be patient. Once rooted, the canopy can be removed and the light level increased, but watering must continue on a fairly consistent basis. With the root system established, the plant can be transplanted into the garden.

Duchesse de Brabant, 1857
Tea

The exquisitely formed roses of 'Duchesse de Brabant' are round like a cabbage, as if pulled from a Dutch Master painting. The real bonus of having 'Duchesse de Brabant' in our gardens, besides her beauty, is the luscious raspberry tea fragrance that is present even in our hot summers. Teddy Roosevelt made this rose his favorite, often wearing it as a boutenniere. This large, memorable rose of carefree habit is one of our favorites too. Flowers fall from the plant before any hint of browning occurs. Grown only as far North as St Louis, Missouri, 'Duchesse de Brabant's' tenderness dictates a Southern home.

An antique cranberry flower vase filled with 'Duchesse de Brabant' and her white sport, 'Madame Joseph Schwartz', is displayed exactly as Teddy Roosevelt would have enjoyed. This was his favorite rose that he often wore on his lapel.

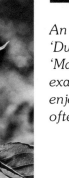

Flowers too heavy to be supported by 'Duchesse de Brabant's' weak stems add to the romantic Victorian quality of this rose.

'Madame Antoine Mari' greets visitors on a walkway leading to the Antique Rose Emporium chapel. Her flowers are often used to provide petals in lieu of rice to shower the bride and groom.

Madame Antoine Mari, 1901
Tea

So perfect is the purity of its color that the buff pink petals of 'Madame Antoine Mari' appear to be porcelain. This makes 'Madame Antoine Mari' a wonderful choice for cut flowers, as well as a garden plant.

Thick heavy foliage on a rather full and rounded bush (as opposed to the other Teas' more erect shape) gives it distinction in our borders. Henry Flowers, designer and consultant for Antique Rose Emporium gardens states, "This is the very best Tea rose that I have grown. It blooms almost constantly."

Marie van Houtte, 1871
Tea

    'Marie van Houtte' and 'Mrs. Dudley Cross' are often confused because their flowers look identical. That is where the similarity stops however. 'Marie von Houtte' tends to grow faster and attain a much larger size than 'Mrs. Dudley Cross' and her canes also have thorns (botanically called prickles). The presence of prickles as well as her massive size (up to 8 feet) dictates her placement at the the back of the perennial border.

Mrs. Dudley Cross, 1907
Tea

Very rarely have we found a cane with thorns on 'Mrs. Dudley Cross.' This and her bi-colored yellow and pink flowers keep her close to walkways, doorways, and highly trafficked areas where her beauty and fragrance can be admired without the danger of a scratch. Found in older gardens throughout the South, 'Mrs. Dudley Cross' perseveres still in today's modern gardens. Like most of the Teas, plants are 4 to 6 feet tall and seldom need pruning except for a bi-annual shaping to maintain the garden scale.

Thorns (prickles) on the stem of 'Marie van Houtte's' flowers differentiate it from 'Mrs. Dudley Cross' which is thornless. Flowers appear to be identical. 'Marie van Houtte' grows faster and larger than 'Mrs. Dudley Cross' at the Antique Rose Emporium display gardens in Texas.

'Mrs. Dudley Cross' is the perfect thornless rose to safely grace the garden where people will be sitting.

Monsieur Tillier, 1891
Tea

This handsome 6-foot-tall Tea rose bears flowers that are a mixture of pale rose, salmon, and purple. From a distance though, the overall color appears to be cherry red. The unusual color of flat, double flowers makes this rose very striking. We have used 'Monsieur Tillier' in hedge rows next to 'Mutabilis' to screen and enclose two unique theme gardens. On one side is a formal allée of perennials backed by a tall rose hedge. On the other is an informal herb garden with serpentine walkways and layered plantings. The rose hedge acts as a wall, keeping the enclosed herb garden uncluttered from distracting views.

Mature vase-shaped roses of 'Monsieur Tillier' (below) are ready for their early spring shaping. Healthy plants like this need only the quick removal of the top 1/3 of the plant. The size of the plant is maintained so that the plant will fit into the proper scale of the garden.

After a severe freeze, shoots emerge from the crown of the plant ensuring its survival (middle right). Grafted roses would be left with only root stock.

On Your Own

Roses grown on their own roots are superior. Plants are grown from cuttings rather than budded or grafted onto rootstocks. As Gertrude Jekyll in her book <u>Roses for English Gardens</u> states, "They are much long-lived, they give more bloom, they bloom more continuously, and they throw up no troublesome suckers. Grafted plants may be best for the production of show blooms, ... whereas own root roses ... fulfill their best purpose as true garden plants." A vegetatively propagated rose means that it is part of the same plant that could have been admired by Pliny, cultivated by a Chinese emperor, grown at Malmaison by Empress Josephine, or carried West by an American pioneer woman. It is this tie with the events of human history that we feel makes the old rose the ultimate antique, unlike a painting or a piece of furniture, the old rose is a living testament to history and man's quest for beauty.

'Monsieur Tillier' and 'Mutabilis' share duties as a hedge. This garden reflects the Hispanic personality and Southwestern flair of San Antonio. Cacti, agave, and other xeriscape perennials are companions to the roses - giving it this authentic interpretation.

Garden Design

An evocative, spell binding garden has good structure (definitive borders, walls, walkways, etc.) and balanced form (symmetry and scale of plantings). These two qualities alone are the "bones" of a good garden allowing seasonal changes of color and texture to evolve within this framework over time. Color is often given the most credit to a particularly beautiful garden, but color is short-lived. A garden must have the longer lasting qualities of structure and balanced form to be effective. Style, contrast, mass, harmony, texture, and shape are all more subtle elements of garden design.

Mrs. B. R. Cant, 1901
Tea

We have more 'Mrs. B. R. Cant' roses planted in our garden than any other rose. It is the rose of choice for a long serpentine hedge on the grounds, and it separates a rose history walk from the open lawn of a Victorian restoration. With its size and stature of 8 feet by 8 feet, it works perfectly. Ironically, the original 'Mrs. B. R. Cant' was planted in front of the Victorian porch and grew too big, thereby dwarfing the garden. Silvery pink flowers are also large, 4 inches across in a flat quartered pattern. The spring flowering, which is usually the heaviest, is breathtaking when mixed with Texas bluebonnets. Mr. Benjamin Cant served his wife well by naming this rose for her.

'Mrs. B. R. Cant' (above) is one of many planted in a 200 foot hedge. Even after a year and half of growth, she fills her space amply with foliage and flowers.

'Mrs. B. R. Cant' soars over other Tea roses near this Victorian porch. Unfortunately, after the fifth year, 'Mrs. B. R. Cant' had to be removed as plants around her were dwarfed by her size.

Safrano, 1839
Tea

'Safrano' is one of our best known Tea roses. Hundred year old specimens have been found on many old graves through the South. The plants we have in our garden came from cuttings from a cemetery in Richmond, Virginia, its northernmost range of hardiness. 'Safrano' is found in New Zealand, Australia, Bermuda, South Africa, and anywhere that a warm climate will support its constant bloom. The upright shape of the bush, along with lovely bright apricot buds that open saffron, make it a perfect specimen where it can really show off. Focal points like the corners of a perennial bed or singly featured specimens in large containers are prime garden locations in which to place 'Safrano'. A light pruning in early spring and early fall stimulates a flush of bronze colored new growth that contrast dramatically with the golden buds. The yellow-flowered sport, 'Isabella Sprunt', was introduced in 1855. Color mutations, or sports, are otherwise exact replicas of the original rose and occur in many varieties.

Care must be taken that Tea roses like 'Safrano', don't get too big, thwarting the gardener's ability to keep it in proper scale with the rest of the garden.

'Safrano' is one of the most durable Tea roses. Many specimens are still surviving in cemeteries throughout the South and Southeast. Here 'Safrano' dwarfs Katie Beltzhoover's grave in Natchez, Mississippi. Cemeteries are very fruitful hunting grounds for time-tested plants. To honor the deceased, loved ones would often plant their favorite rose or iris. Many years later these plants still adorn the grave. Along with obtaining permission to take cuttings of these plants, extreme care must be taken so that these original plants continue to grace these sites for years to come.

A Palette of Teas

The following Tea roses are equally as beautiful and useful to the Southern garden as those profiled on prior pages.

Working counter-clockwise from the top left page these roses are: 'Madame Berkeley', 'Madame Antoine Rebe', 'Mlle. Franziska Krüger', 'Perle des Jardins', 'Dr. Grill', 'G. Nabonnand', 'Maman Cochet' and 'Frances Dubreuil.'

Belinda's Dream, 1992
Shrub

We began growing this plant as "Belinda's Rose" in 1987. Dr. Robert Basye, in his quest for breeding disease resistance, thornlessness, and beauty into modern roses, had produced a seedling from a cross between 'Tiffany' and 'Jersey Beauty'. Though certainly not an end to his admirable quest, he named this plant "Belinda's Rose" after the daughter of one of his friends. "Belinda's Rose" is a fast growing shrub, upright and sturdy with few disease problems. High-centered, distinctively fragrant, pink flowers are produced freely throughout the growing season. "Belinda's Rose" was renamed 'Belinda's Dream' in 1992 when registered with the American Rose Society. This rose has been picked by the Texas Agricultural Extension Service's CEMAP (Coordinated Educational and Marketing Assistance Program) as an excellent plant. 'Belinda's Dream' will be promoted as one of the best garden roses in Texas in 2002. This deserved recognition is a fitting tribute to Dr. Basye.

'Belinda's Dream' flourishes in an enclosed Mexican courtyard in San Antonio. Fountains, pots, and rustic furniture help convey the Hispanic flavor of this garden. Tropical yellow flowered daturas and palo verdes compliment the setting.

Carol Kiphart shares her chair with 'Belinda's Dream' roses that were arranged by Jim Johnson of the Benz School of Floral Design.

'Belinda's Dream' adds beauty and continuity to this perennial border beside a country home in Texas. Native perennials which are the companions to these roses are Penstemon tenuifolia, Salvia farinacea, and iris.

103

Graham Thomas™, 1983
Shrub

'Graham Thomas' is one of David Austin's English roses. He introduced it in 1983 and trademarked the name after the British old rose expert, Graham Stuart Thomas. The plant produces bright yellow roses with the old rose shape, flat and quartered in the center. The fragrance is unusual and spicy. Because it is rather upright, many gardeners are at a loss as how to control this rose. We have heard numerous remedies of either pruning back hard, pegging, or training it as a small climber. Any way, it looks magnificent in the garden. The rose is hardy in zone 5 and warmer. If grown as a shrub it should be pruned twice a year where its best kept height is 4 to 5 feet. If trained as a pillar rose or on a trellis, only occasional thinning is required to achieve an 8 foot mannerly climber.

'Graham Thomas' adds to the explosion of color in this perennial border. The bird feeder acts as a focal point giving stability to the busy scene. The colorful companions are butterfly bush (Buddlea), Salvia leucantha, *orange mums and yellow violas. The purple foliage plants are ornamental peppers.*

Heritage™, 1983
Shrub

'Heritage' is one of David Austin's earlier English Rose introductions. She is the best performing English rose at the Antique Rose Emporium gardens in both Brenham and San Antonio. Cabbagey, soft pink, fragrant flowers repeat throughout the entire season. These flowers are embellished by the clean bluish-green foliage. 'Heritage' is cold hardy growing happily in zone 5 or warmer. She is a wonderful cut flower and is ideally suited for centerpieces to adorn your dining room table.

'Heritage' reflects the serenity and purity exemplified by the religious statue. Roses reflect on the personality of a setting depending on garden ornaments like sculpture, statues, and yard art that are employed by the gardener. Appropriate companion plants complete this interpretation.

Katy Road Pink
Found

Surviving roses found in older neighborhoods, cemeteries, and abandoned homesites, in addition to their enduring quality, often have other assets that make them great garden plants for our modern gardens. Numbers of these roses were collected by the Antique Rose Emporium in the 1980s. Old catalogs and books were helpful in identifying some roses, but many still remain a mystery. They simply remained found roses and were sold as such. Names like "Odee Pink", "Caldwell Pink", "Mary Minor", and "San Marcos Red" were names given to these roses. Some shared the names of the generous homeowners who gave us cuttings, some from the area where they were found, and some describing what the rose looked like. Those roses that performed with outstanding bloom and fragrance were put into the Antique Rose Emporium's early catalogue and sold so that others could enjoy their beauty. Dr. and Mrs. Stahl of Houston shared this rose with us which was found in Katy, Texas. "Katy Road Pink" is very floriferous, with new very long buds appearing at all times during the growing season. The graceful 5-foot plant with gray-green foliage seldom has insect or disease problems.

The entrance to the Texas cottage garden features the combination of "Katy Road Pink" with Baby Blue Eyes and Mealy Blue Sage.

"Katy Road Pink's" shockingly bright flowers add life to this gray container and liven up the walkways in this San Antonio garden. Oversized 30-inch containers can support large roses like this rose.

Lafter, 1948
Hybrid Tea

This is another rose shared with us by Dr. Basye. He evaluated many roses with the idea of breeding for disease resistance. 'Lafter' was one of the few Hybrid Teas that passed the grade. His rose beds were never sprayed nor nurtured. Plants that looked good did so because they had the genetic fortitude to succeed without the aid of chemical sprays or constant feeding. 'Lafter' grows fast, stays green and healthy, and has bright orange-pink long stemmed flowers that modern breeders admire in roses. The plant looks at home in our garden, where the orange flowers are mixed with blue and violet perennials.

Bright colors of the Hybrid Tea roses show why they are known for their exhibition quality. The roses used are 'Lafter' (orange), 'Mrs. Oakley Fisher' (yellow), 'Radiance' (pink), 'Chrysler Imperial' (red), 'Aloha' (pink), 'Dame de Coeur' (red), and 'Mrs. Pierre S. Dupont' (yellow).

The use of white hot daisies, bright orange 'Lafter' roses, and yellow columbine are arranged to make this floral arrangement appear like shooting stars, which it was aptly named.

The rectilinear architecture of the chapel, and straight rectangular beds lining the walkways provide the rigid framework for drifts of perennials, grasses, roses, and annuals. Repetition gives this border rhythm and continuity as visitors approach. Orange, yellow and white flowers of the plantings are especially well suited for this autumnal scene.

Maggie
Found

"Maggie" is a versatile shrub rose. Her long canes can be trained on a trellis or pillar or pruned to make a large shrub. Regardless of its garden form, "Maggie's" greatest gift is her flower. Magenta red, flat, quartered flowers with a spicy rose scent akin to the roses in the Bourbon class occur heavily in spring and then again in the fall. "Maggie" is a found rose named by Dr. William C. Welch. He named it for his wife's grandmother who bought it at the turn of the century. "Maggie", the rose, is now a registered name with the American Rose Society. Original identities of such roses can be very difficult to ascertain. Faded color photographs and old descriptions from books and catalogues are often ambiguous. This rose, undoubtedly, was very popular. It is still found in older gardens or cemeteries throughout the South and even on the island of Bermuda where it is called "Pacifica", a name they coined much earlier.

"I'm still alive today because I work in my yard everyday." That's what Mattie Breedlove told me when I visited her garden in 1988. An earthen swept yard, characteristic of an African culture was maintained to minimize fire danger and vermin from encroaching on the house, is still evident in her garden in Central Texas. Plants like the rose "Maggie", Crinum lilies, and iris are all pass-along plants that originated generations earlier. Both culture and plants are glimpses into the past.

Cemeteries located throughout the region offer visitors a glimpse of our horticultural past. Some plants planted 100 years ago still survive, offering the modern homeowner a time tested-example of the plants that will do well in this area. Shown are peonies and iris in a Denver, Colorado, cemetery. Palm trees and crepe myrtles are seen in a Charleston, South Carolina, cemetery.

Found Roses

Rose-rustling is gaining recognition lately and deservedly so. The title rose-rustling, albeit rather illicit sounding is actually admirable in its purpose. Rustling is another name for the search and rescue of lost and forgotten roses that may have otherwise been lost to commerce altogether. These plants were once popular in the cottage gardens and estates of the 18th and 19th centuries where they flourished as fragrant landscape plants. Rose rustling will ensure their preservation for future generations.

A newly found rose cannot positively be identified, but this should not diminish its value. Many foundlings are given study names until their true identity can be established. Roses with names like 'Martha Gonzales', "Old Gay Hill Red China", "Highway 290 Pink Buttons" and "Odee Pink" are coined by the rustlers in an effort to document the initial find. These names describe either the location of the found rose or the person who shared the cutting. These roses will not be found in literature under these "study" names, however they are plants that still offer a gardener much pleasure. Because of their versatility, they provide an alternative to many of the short lived modern shrubs seen today. Most collectors can use a reference library of old catalogues and books and rely on the aid of experienced rosarians in an effort to determine the true identity of these foundlings. 'Old Blush', with its constant bloom and carefree habit, the fragrant Sweetbriar Rose of Shakespeare's "A Midsummer's Night Dream", and 'Louise Philippe', the deep red China rose thought to have been brought over by Lorenzo de Zavala, the first Texas statesman as minister to France, are examples of what has been found.

Surviving roses are found in these places, old cemeteries, the overgrown yards of abandoned homes, and the lush viable gardens of green-thumbed homeowners who have a passion for collecting and growing anything and everything, including their grandmother's favorite rose.

Each of these locations provides us with a glimpse of the past, a living testament to what once was popular and admired in past times. These places are mini-arboretums of time-tested plants, and therefore a true reflection of a gardener's successes over time. Under the strict laws of nature wherein only the strong survive, a rustler is tantalized with a selection of plants that has withstood these tests. As anyone living in Texas can attest, the "blue northers" of winter and long droughts of summer will test any plant's ability to survive.

A good scout on the hunt for time-tested roses has good success in cemeteries. The best cemeteries are not necessarily the biggest and best kept since the lawnmower and weedeater can be a plant's worst enemy. Policies in many cemeteries now ensure that only grass is to be planted. Trees, shrubs, roses and perennial plantings on headstones which once served as a living testament to the affection between the living and departed are now forbidden in many cemeteries.

Southern cemeteries primarily yield old fashioned, everblooming Tea and China roses dating back to the mid 1800s. It is interesting to note that Texas nurseryman, Thomas Affleck, one of the most respected authorities on farming and gardening in the nation during the 1850s, sold 270 named varieties of roses throughout the South and East. Could it be that roses found today near headstones dating back to that period were from these offerings?

Even ethnic influence and historic interest can be seen in the plantings of small town cemeteries. German towns in central Texas like Schulenburg and Brenham share the same red roses that certainly must have been passed around within the community. An old cemetery of predominant Mexican influence in San Marcos is full of red and yellow flowers exemplifying their cultural preferences for the bright and cheerful colors. The link between culture and plants is seen by the flora that adorns these ethnic cemeteries.

The greatest joy of rose rustling, though, comes from visiting with the older self-taught gardeners that still reside in original frame homes where they have happily gardened for years. These people usually live in the less affluent neighborhoods and older parts of town. A good scout will avoid the homes that have the characteristic "mustache landscape" (hedge of privet or boxwood that surrounds the foundation or footing of the house). He will keep a keen eye for those yards dotted with numerous trees and shrubs of all varieties which are the indicators of homeowners with a passion for gardening. Here we find generous individuals like Mary Minor, Martha Gonzales, Mrs. Odee, and Mattie Breedlove, all of whom have gardened in the ways of their parents and grandparents. These individuals are self taught gardeners whose experience could never be passed down in books. They often turn their backs to the newest varieties that fill up the garden centers and grow and share what has been in their family for years. At first, apprehensive about the rustler's visit, they quickly succumb to the euphoria that addiction to plants and their discussion brings. It's not long before the rustler is invited in and ultimately ushered to the backyard where the real family treasures are found. Cuttings of roses are shared and stories are told. From these encounters we learn of "willow water" and its miraculous ability to root cuttings that are soaked in it. Wives' tales abound yet beautiful plants of numerous varieties attest to their magic.

So now as I walk into my garden amongst my found roses, I see Mattie Breedlove, Martha Gonzales, and Mrs. Odee; so diverse are the personalities and warm are the acquaintances that their memories are more sweet than the fragrances of the roses themselves.

• •

The following groups were organized to share their interest in old roses. Members meet monthly to discuss the collection, preservation, and identification of old roses. Newsletters are also published.

Charles A. Walker, Jr.
Heritage Rose Foundation
1512 Gorman Street
Raleigh, NC 27606-2919

(A non-profit corporation devoted exclusively to the preservation and study of heritage roses.)

Dallas Area Historical Rose Group
P O Box 38585
Dallas, TX 75238-0585

Texas Rose Rustlers
c/o Shannon Sherrod
Route 1, Box 1005
Chireno, TX 75937

• • • • • • • • • • • • • • • •

Texas Rose Rustlers care for a rose in a Texas cemetery (left). At an annual gathering, cuttings of roses are shared so that these plants will continue to be passed down and enjoyed for generations to come.

Marchessa Boccella, 1842
Hybrid Perpetual

The Hybrid Perpetuals are the class of roses that represented man's quest for larger, long stemmed roses. They are the precursors to the modern Hybrid Teas. Over 4000 varieties were introduced during the period 1837–1900. The name "perpetual" doesn't necessarily imply that all these roses repeat their bloom throughout the season. Most do not. We consider 'Marchessa Boccella', 'Paul Neyron', (the giant cabbage rose), 'Reine des Violets', and 'Baronne Prevost' the best of the class because they do repeat their bloom. 'Marchessa Boccella' has large, quartered, very fragrant flowers that rest virtually atop the foliage on short stems . We have seen beautiful specimens in gardens throughout the United States.

This backyard potting shed named "Nutshell" houses white doves and supports Old Garden Roses. 'Marchessa Boccella' in the foreground exhibits her characteristic upright form and bountiful flowers.

The Living Soil

The development and maintenance of a good garden is dependent on the management of the soil. Roses old and new do best in a well prepared bed incorporated with lots of organic matter. It is rare to see our native forests in a state of starvation. Mother Nature has ensured that these plants grow and stay green without the aid of man's synthetic fertilizers. The constant decomposition of leaf litter, dead branches, and bark that falls to the ground in these areas provide nutrition. This organic matter provides food for bacteria and fungi, nematodes and protozoa, the byproducts of which provide all the nutrients and minerals necessary for the forest to thrive. Other symbiotic relationships between plants and fungi enable the plants to drink water and obtain necessary minerals.

The gardener would do well if he could mimic this in his garden. Good results have been achieved using the following guidelines: Mixing 2 to 3 inches of decomposed organic matter like composted leaves or manure into 6 to 8 inches of soil. The soil can be composed of clay, sand, loam, or silt. Roses and perennials should be planted in this mixture and mulched with 2 to 3 inches of coarser material like hardwood bark. Mulch will slowly decompose, providing a continual source of food for fungi and bacteria, creating a living and nutritive soil. The addition of more mulch biannually insures the continuation of this process. The advantages, besides not having to apply synthetic fertilizers, are numerous. Beds retain moisture, the pH of the soil is buffered, weeds are kept at bay, soil temperatures fluctuate less, and the appearance is better.

Penelope, 1924
Hybrid Musk

'Penelope' is one of Joseph Pemberton's most popular introductions. Unlike the other Hybrid Musks featured in the cascading climbers, 'Penelope' is a large upright shrub with stiff twiggy canes. Plants are 4 to 5 feet tall and wide, perfect for making hedges. She bears dense corymbs of very pale, salmon pink flowers of strong aroma followed by a winter crop of large pink hips. 'Penelope' is useful also as a specimen at the back of a perennial border or isolated in a large pot. Its versatility and cold hardiness (zone 5) make it one of the most widely used in the Pemberton collection.

A Shady Deal

An important caveat to mention before attempting to grow roses in shade is that roses do better in full sun. Knowing this, any success of growing roses in shade is based on how much light the rose gets in the shade. In any given garden, ranges of light intensity vary from full sun to pockets of shade. Shade can vary from light to dense depending on shadows cast by walls or overhangs. Under no circumstances would a rose do well in a heavy shaded area. Bright open areas under the shade of tall trees can offer enough light to grow some varieties of roses like the 'Swamp Rose' and Hybrid Musk roses without jeopardizing their contribution of flower and form. At least six hours of direct sun (morning or afternoon) a day is required for optimum performance. Decreasing the exposure of sun proportionally decreases the quality of bloom, the number of flowers, the foliage density, the health of the foliage, and the size and form of the bush. Remarkably, roses perform better in full sun, even in extremely hot areas like Central Texas westward to Arizona, on a year-round basis than those that have less sun exposure.

This allée of pear trees is underplanted with 'Penelope' roses. The development of the garden from winter to spring shows the ability of this rose to grow and bloom under the shade of small trees. Roses in the foreground have much more sun exposure than those under the canopy of the trees. This accounts for 'Penelope's' larger size and bloom here.

Puerto Rico
Found

"Puerto Rico" was a rose shared with us from Jose Marrero, a Puerto Rican, via Mrs. Cleo Barnwell (a Louisiana collector and gardener extraordinaire). As the case with many found roses, this rose was also found growing in other locations. Cuttings of a rose from Bermuda named "Maitland White", were also shared with us and proved to be the same rose. Regardless of the names, this rose bears much similarity to early Hybrid Tea roses in form and fragrance. "Puerto Rico" has a narrow erect habit to 6 feet, bearing long stemmed flowers that are creamy white with a hint of apricot pink. The plant is not only incredibly useful in the garden, where it softens the foundations of an old homestead, but also as a luscious cut flower. "Puerto Rico" is tender and ranges only into zone 6 only with protection. We have found that pruning heavily and shaping this rose improves bloom in spring and fall.

Shiny foliage on an erect, vase-shaped bush with creamy white flowers held high on long stems are clues that indicate that "Puerto Rico" is probably a Hybrid Tea introduced at the turn of the century. Such roses that still survive today are great contributors to modern gardens even if their originally introduced name is not known.

Souvenir de la Malmaison, 1843
Bourbon

Thomas Affleck, a Texas nurseryman, in 1856 stated, "How I envy the grower who first saw that plant bloom, the seed of which he had sown, feeling that such a gem was his!" 'Souvenir de la Malmaison' produces large, flat, quartered blossoms with thick petals of a flesh pink. We have found that the plant can grow to almost 6 feet, if left unpruned, but it is best kept at 3 to 4 feet. This compact size intensifies the number of flowers relative to the size of the bush.

'Souvenir de la Malmaison', a representative of the Bourbon class, has gorgeous fragrant flowers for which they are known. But unlike those in the class, she is a shapely, free-standing shrub that needs little care save for being a little susceptible to black spot. Many other Bourbon roses like 'Madame Isaac Pereire' and 'Variegata di Bologna' are open, leggy shrubs that are useful only if pegged or trained vertically.

Empress Josephine, wife of Napolean, lived at Malmaison where her passion of collecting roses flourished. Unfortunately, Empress Josephine never knew this lovely rose as she died in 1814. It was simply named in honor of her garden.

What a Sport!

Mother Nature has an interesting way of increasing the diversity of our rose offerings. They are genetic mutations called sports. Changes in the flower color, the number of petals in a flower, the form of the plant (climbing form vs. bush form), and variegation of foliage are some possible manifestations resulting from these mutations. They occur as sudden changes to a particular part of a plant. Cuttings taken from these mutated canes will maintain this new form.

'Souvenir de la Malmaison' shown on the right side of the photo has many sports. A white-colored sport named 'Kronprincessin Viktoria' and a less double form called 'Souvenir de St Anne's' are pictured here. There are other sports like a vigorous climbing form and a red flowering form. They are all genetically the same, save for a single trait expression.

IV
Small Shrubs

Small Shrubs

Basye's Blueberry
Blush Noisette
Caldwell Pink
Cecile Brunner
Dame de Coeur
Ducher
Eutin
Grüss an Aachen
Hermosa
Highway 290 Pink Buttons

Iceberg
Kirsten Poulsen
La Marne
Marie Pavié
Martha Gonzales
Mrs. R. M. Finch
Perle d 'Or
Rise 'n' Shine
The Fairy

Basye's Blueberry, 1982
Shrub

The erect growth habit, rounded leaves, thornless stems, and fall coloration of 'Basye's Blueberry' make it look quite similar to a blueberry bush. Bright pink, semi-double, fragrant flowers with bright yellow stamens add to its appeal. This plant represents one of the stepping stones towards Dr. Robert Basye's goal of thornless, disease-free roses. The plant is our most prolific seed producer, covering itself with orange hips in the fall and winter. This tendency makes it a breeder's answer when searching for a fertile mother plant. This tough, carefree shrub tolerates neglect and aggressive companions such as verbena and violets.

Hips containing the seeds of the
rose are prized for their high
vitamin C content. 'Basye's
Blueberry' is known for these small
apple-like hips. Their color and
form make them beautiful fall
garden ornaments as well as food
for wildlife.

Blush Noisette, 1817
Noisette

Unlike the lion's share of Noisettes that make vigorous romantic climbers, 'Blush Noisette' is a small billowing shrub of 3 to 5 feet with equal spread. Some gardeners have reported its use as a pillar rose, but we have never found it growing to a height to make the proper statement as a pillar. Using it as a soft foundation plant or container rose is more natural for its form. After John Champneys had produced 'Champneys' Pink Cluster' by crossing 'Old Blush' and a Musk rose from Shakespeare's days, he gave it to a friend, Philippe Noisette, who crossed it with a Tea rose producing 'Blush Noisette' in 1817. The French, favoring the wonderful fragrance and clustering blooms, expanded the class to large flowering forms like 'Reve d'Or', 'Lamarque', and 'Madame Alfred Carrière'. Because of their vigor and tenderness to cold, the Noisettes were immensely popular and well adapted to the Southern states. The Noisettes are the aristocrats of the South, creating a romantic period effect unlike any other rose.

'Blush Noisette' shines in the early morning sun, flourishing in the Antique Rose Emprorium herb garden.

'Blush Noisette', draped with white flowers,
gives no relief to the figurine needing
warmth, not beauty.

'Champneys' Pink Cluster'
with clematis shares the rails
of a stairway to this house in
northern Georgia. It was the
first Noisette rose that
eventually led to many other
varieties, including 'Blush
Noisette'.

Caldwell Pink
Found

Texas, like most Gulf Coast areas, has summers where temperature and humidity are so oppressive that even the China and Tea roses rest after their heavy spring blooms. "Caldwell Pink" is the exception to this rule. In March, April, and early May, when our gardens are at peak bloom, "Caldwell Pink" is just getting started. Massive clusters of flowers in shades of pink stop traffic in June when the rest of the garden is starting to broil. Plants are best kept at 3 to 5 feet with the help of aggressive shearing, as an unchecked plant could reach 6 feet. Besides the summer bloom that extends into October, this rose rewards us with wonderful fall color. Red, orange, purple, and yellow leaves form on frost touched plants in time to brighten the garden once again. "Caldwell Pink" was discovered in Caldwell, Texas by Tommy Adams, a propagator for Antique Rose Emporium at the time. Some suspect this rose to be "Pink Pet". It is definitely one of our best time-tested survivors for the hot Southern garden.

"Caldwell Pink's" autumnal colors of red, orange, and yellow are as dramatic in fall as they are in spring, despite the absence of flowers.

An unusual mix of colors are seen here with the pink flowers of "Caldwell Pink" and the fluorescent orange perennial, Tecoma stans, in this arid Texas garden.

"Caldwell Pink" and Texas sage grow well together, even blooming at similar times in the hot Texas climate.

Cecile Brunner, 1881
Polyantha

This famous rose, better known as the "Sweetheart Rose", should be in every garden. Roses in the Polyantha class are hardy, disease resistant, and floriferous. Most of them are compact, even dwarf, like modern miniatures, and they lend themselves well to low borders, mass plantings, or containers. We use them in mass to stabilize mixed plantings and in drifts to unify the diverse plantings in long borders and beds. The gardener that has a small area like a patio, porch, or even a rooftop garden will find Polyanthas like 'Cecile Brunner' the ideal size to fit the scale of these gardens. Her shell pink, perfectly formed flowers are very fragrant. They were often used as boutonnieres for loved ones to wear on their lapels.

A spray of 'Cecile Brunner' is artistically tied to 'Belinda's Dream' roses in this evocative arrangement designed by Jim Johnson of the Benz School of Floral Design.

The red flowers of 'Dame de Coeur' break up the softer hues of surrounding Tea roses.

Dame de Coeur, 1958
Hybrid Tea

This small rose is a resulting cross of two larger Hybrid Tea roses, 'Peace' and 'Independence'. Staying compact at 3 to 4 feet, it is ideally suited for use in containers and low borders. Known as the "Black Rose", 'Dame de Coeur's' cherry red blooms darken to a magenta crimson as it ages. The blue undertones of this vibrant red rose allow it to mix well in the garden with other perennials and old roses. It makes a great cut flower and, unlike most Hybrid Teas, has a fragrance.

Ducher, 1869
China

We feel this China rose belongs within this group of small shrubs, although some might argue that specimens have grown to over 6 feet. Its best kept size is 3 to 4 feet where it can embelish the foundation of small structures, like pump houses, greenhouses, or storage sheds. We've used it in containers and have also found that it makes a great specimen in small perennial beds. 'Ducher's' pure white flowers, rare for the China class, are fragrant and showy. The compact, dense habit and smaller form allow the flowers to better show against the darker background. Without this foil, other white roses seem lost in the bright glare of the sky. We can count on 'Ducher' to be the first rose to bloom in the spring.

'Ducher', one of the few white Chinas, fills this terra cotta pot at the Antique Rose Emporium gardens in San Antonio.

A pavé composed of China roses, 'Green Rose', 'Old Blush', 'Louis Philippe', 'Archduke Charles', and 'Ducher', in a Flexible Flyer wagon adds whimsical interest for a social function in the garden.

Eutin, 1940
Floribunda

For years we grew a found rose called "Rustler's Skyrocket". Rose expert and grower of old garden roses in Australia, David Ruston, when visiting our gardens was asked if he knew the rose. He remarked "There's no disputin', it's 'Eutin'", thereby ending the "Rustler's Skyrocket" identity crisis. 'Eutin' is a small cascading shrub to 4 feet. Flower heads can be as large as basketballs with some 50 to 60 individual flowers. There are stunning examples of this rose by many old Texas homes, growing in very poor conditions. We love it as a container rose, for the heavy flowers pull canes over the edge and down the sides of the pot. It's extremely hardy and blooms prolifically in the fall.

The red roses of 'Eutin', 'Général Jacqueminot', 'Souvenir de Docteur Jamain', and 'Granny Grimmets' ground the arrangement and balance the vertical elements of the Jacob's Ladder and willow.

Plume Crazy

Many of the Southern old garden roses are heavy bloomers in the fall. This aspect posed with the ornamental plume grasses, which is also the most dramatic in fall, provides the gardener with a stunning combination. Ornamental grasses come in many colors and combine with roses of all hues. Their graceful, linear growth habit — tufted, mounded, arching, and upright offers a refreshing contrast to the more rounded shape of roses and their blooms. Combinations with roses are endless, but the architectural feature offered by the form and texture of grass is still untapped by modern gardeners. The brick red inflorescence of *Muhlenbergia capillaris* provides a feathery backdrop for white flowered roses like 'Iceberg' and 'Jeanne d'Arc'. A sensational monochromatic display is seen with the red flowers of 'Eutin' and this grass.

Grüss an Aachen, 1909
Floribunda

Generally credited as the first Floribunda, 'Grüss an Aachen' is considered also by some to be the best. A cross between a dwarf China rose, 'Rouletii' and *R. multiflora* led to the ever-blooming class of small roses called Polyanthas. These Polyanthas were then crossed with some larger flowering Teas giving rise to the Floribundas. As you might expect, their larger flowers on compact plants, enabled them to be showier in the landscape. 'Grüss an Aachen' has 3-inch flowers of multi-colored pink, yellow, and buff borne on a 3-to 4-foot

graceful shrub. Used either in mass or singly for accent, there are few roses that can rival it. 'Grüss an Aachen' is hardy and remontant and makes a good choice for Southern and Northern gardens alike.

The pink form of 'Grüss an Aachen' follows a grass walkway on one side while an mixed border hides a makeshift storage building on the other.

Hermosa, 1840
China

'Hermosa' is a small and compact China rose that makes a 3-to 4-foot shrub. Flowers are full and cabbagey, reminiscent of the Bourbon roses and their Damask parentage. Blue-green foliage on a dense twiggy bush contrasts with the mauve-pink flowers. Famed Southern nursery-man Thomas Affleck of Natchez, Mississippi, and Gay Hill, Texas, said of Hermosa in 1856, "Still one of the best … and nearly always in bloom." A century and a half later, we can still agree with his assessment. We've put 'Hermosa' in a whiskey barrel near a walkway intersection in our garden. We are not the least bit amazed by the attention and praise she receives from our visitors.

Shearing back container roses promotes thick, chunky shrubs and keeps them in proportion to the size of the pot.

'Hermosa' (right) is poised atop other 24-inch whiskey barrels to create a unique display. The benefit of container growing is seen in the ability to move a plant from one part of the garden to another thereby creating changeable expressions.

Contain Yourself

For the homeowner who does not have the luxury of space, growing roses in pots is the best way to garden. Whether gardening on patios, porches, or roofs, the mobility of plants is the biggest container growing advantage. Plants can be moved in order to capture the best sunlight as well as brought indoors, temporarily adding color and fragrance for a special indoor event.

Pots come in an infinite number of styles, colors, and sizes. Growing roses in pots does require some added cultural requirements that landscape plants do not. Soil or media should provide additional aeration and drainage capacities. Store bought potting soils are usually mixtures of peat, decomposed bark, vermiculite, and perlite. They are prefered to top soils and sand-based soils that are heavy and tend to compact. Water and fertilizers which are more naturally available to plants growing in the ground must be added to container grown plants. Slow release fertilizers containing micro-nutrients provide long lasting fertility and are safer to use than water soluble fertilizers. Too much or too little water or fertilizer or excessive heat and cold can kill plants in containers. The gardener must be more attentive to potted plants in order to be successful.

Roses that stay below 3 feet of height are perfect candidates for container culture. Pots 16 to 24 inches wide and 12 to 24 inches deep can support the roses for many years. Occasional pruning in early spring and fall will keep these roses full and shapely. When and if temperatures drop below 20 below Fahrenheit container plants should be moved to protected areas so that the root mass does not freeze.

Highway 290 Pink Buttons
Found

Of all the roses that the Antique Rose Emporium has grown names like "The Hole Rose", "Red Burglar Rose", "Seguin College Street Pink", "Baptist Manse", and "Old Gay Hill Red China", the one that still gets the most response from her name is "Highway 290 Pink Buttons". Tracking where initial cuttings and shared plants originated takes a lot of creative nomenclature. "Highway 290 Pink Buttons" leaves no doubt as to where we found the plant, nor what the diminutive flowers look like. Mature plants are 18 inches tall and 1 foot wide. Pink, semi-double flowers occur continuously through the season.

The design elements of line, structure and symetry are strengthened by the absence of color in this snow covered garden. "Highway 290 Pink Buttons's" small size lends itself nicely to a border around the sundial.

Iceberg, 1958
Floribunda

This rose is an outstanding addition to any garden. It is very versatile and can be grown as a hedge or specimen. The sweetly scented pure white flowers are wonderful to cut and bring indoors for arrangements.

This rose is a recent addition to our garden. In the short time we have grown this rose, 'Iceberg's' wonderful garden qualities assured its inclusion in this book. We've placed her along an allée leading to a chapel where her pristine beauty reflects the integrity of the building. Combinations with other white flowered plants like mist flower and yarrow add texture and depth to the purity theme.

'Iceberg' roses peek from behind a bench along a herbaceous border featuring grasses, daylilies, and other roses. The installation of the border only one year earlier, is shown at left. In this view, the bed is characterized by evenly spaced groupings of the young plants. Note the white 'Iceberg' roses at the end of the allée.

Kirsten Poulsen, 1924
Floribunda

'Kirsten Poulsen' makes an erect bush to 4 feet. Her bright red flowers are held high above the foliage which gives added emphasis to her position in the garden. Abundant displays of the vivid single flowers are seen throughout the season especially in spring and fall. Mass plantings in drifts are effective and dramatic. 'Kirsten Poulsen' is an all around good rose performing well in both Southern and Northern gardens. 'Betty Prior', a Floribunda known primarily in the North, is a seedling from 'Kirsten Poulsen'.

'Kirsten Poulsen's' bright rosy-red colors mix with 'Betty Prior' and found rose "Phalaenopsis", making for a festive entry to this Georgia garden.

'La Marne', planted as a colorful hedge,
borders this driveway in Atlanta, Georgia.
'Cl Pinkie' frames the garage and brings
balance to 'La Marne' in color and weight.

144

La Marne, 1915
Polyantha

With a consistent show of flowers, 'La Marne' is one of our best performers in the South. Her cupped, semi-double flowers are spread evenly throughout the bush. Even without pruning, 'La Marne' still retains a very compact form with an abundance of natural branching. Bronze new growth is evident through the interior and top of the shrub. Flower buds occur at the end of all these flushes of new growth, accounting for this uniform show of color. Our hot summers fade the pink flowers to almost pure white, but when temperatures drop in the spring and fall, they darken once again. We use the 3-to 4-feet tall bush to create mid-sized borders or singly as a specimen in borders, beds, and pots. 'La Marne' is fragrant and hardy making it one of the best roses for a first time gardener.

Marie Pavié, 1888
Polyantha

Beautiful white flowers on a thornless, compact bush make 'Mavie Pavié' an ideal landscape plant. The delicate, pink buds open to sweetly scented white flowers which appear in clusters

throughout the growing season. The 3-to 4-foot bush is dense with healthy dark-green foliage that acts as an excellent foil to the bright white flowers. Whether used as a specimen, in a container rose, or in a border, this rose has limitless uses in the garden.

The thornless white 'Marie Pavié' roses are perfect as pillows while 'Martha Gonzales' passionate red flowers make a festive coverlet for this bed of roses .

A stone kitchen, restored with porches and picket fence, begs for a period (1850-1900s) cottage garden and perennial border. The completed garden integrates native plants, old roses, and perennials like salvias, penstemons, and assorted iris, as well as annuals that the original homeowner might have planted. The curve of the garden walkway is accented by the showy display of 'Marie Pavié'.

Martha Gonzales, 1984
China

'Martha Gonzales' was a Found rose, shared with us by a Navasota, Texas gardener of the same name. The rose's ease of care and garden success, as touted by other gardeners, spread 'Martha Gonzales's' popularity through the landscape industry. She was so popular that she was registered with the American Rose Society. Sadly, Martha Gonzales passed away in 1999, however, this rose continues to be a living tribute to this generous lady. This colorful rose not only has bright semi-double red flowers, but beautiful reddish-purple new growth which is typical to Chinas. The bush is compact to 2 1/2 feet and works well for massing or creating low borders.

Martha Gonzales (1921–1999) poses in her yard with her prized possessions – roses. 'Martha Gonzales', the rose, was named after her and is now registered with the American Rose Society. This is a fitting tribute for such a generous lady.

We've placed this very special China, 'Martha Gonzales', in a knot garden surrounding a sundial where there are no regrets in the passing of time. Small plants are perfect here so as not to cast a shadow on the sundial. Long allées under rose-covered arches also extend the theme of time (thyme).

'Martha Gonzales' borders a small garden featuring a sculpture with falling water. Sounds, like that of running water, are as important to some gardens as are the sounds of wind, birds, and insects.

Mrs. R. M. Finch, 1923
Polyantha

This Polyantha rose is extremely vigorous and will outgrow its best kept height of 3 to 4 feet if left unchecked. Large trusses of cupped, semi-double, bright, rose pink blooms, occur in mass during spring and fall. Flowers fade slightly as they age, blurring pinks to white as in an impressionist's painting. We utilized its intense show of color around a gazebo, a focal point of our garden. Her size, color, and shape allows 'Mrs. R. M. Finch' to mix easily with other roses, yarrow, hollyhock, and salvia.

'Mrs. R. M. Finch' accents a stairway to the gazebo. 'Cl. Pinkie', trained on rails, adds vertical interest while purple verbena smothers the ground below.

Perle d'Or, 1884
Polyantha

'Perle d'Or' is very similar to the "Sweetheart Rose", 'Cecile Brunner'. So similar it is that we have heard it erroneously called the "Yellow Sweetheart Rose". Apricot, salmon, and peach are colors that better describe it though. Like 'Cecile Brunner', it has good fragrance and beautifully formed buds perfect for boutonnieres. We keep it at 3 to 4 feet in pots or in massed groupings and drifts. Blue-flowered perennials make striking companions with this rose.

Mass plantings of 'Perle d'Or' screens the view of the parking lot on the other side.

A pavé of mixed flowers, seed and fruit, fill a concrete bird bath. Such arrangements are miniature gardens in themselves, possessing color, texture, and form. Elements are (starting at top) blue flowered plumbago, 'Rise 'n' Shine' roses, Mexican coneflowers, pomegranate fruit, barberry, Country Girl mums, 'Red Cascade' roses, purple coneflowers, Nandina berries, 'Souvenir de la Malmaison' roses, and a sunflower seed head.

We've planted 'Rise 'n' Shine' in pots, backed by a gray building. This simple arrangement has inspired visitors for years.

Rise 'n' Shine, 1977
Miniature

'Rise 'n' Shine' is a miniature introduced by Ralph Moore. It has been included in this book because it has wonderful garden qualities that distinguish it from other miniatures. The plant stays very compact without much pruning. Flowers are bright yellow, fading to butter-yellow in hotter temperatures. Its dwarf habit and bright flowers provide a vibrant accent to any border or mass plantings. On bright sunny days, yellow is the first color the viewer sees, creating an illusion of space and depth.

The Fairy, 1932
Polyantha

'The Fairy' is our most popular rose. A favorite with many local landscapers, 'The Fairy's' small habit of 2 feet tall and 4 to 5 feet wide, allows large areas to be covered in color. It is also one of our hardiest roses, successfully growing in areas where temperatures can drop to −20 degrees Fahrenheit. This rose's graceful draping habit, fine glossy green leaves and abundant clusters of pink flowers reinforce its popularity. We use it primarily in mass plantings and borders, however, it looks lovely cascading out of containers too.

'The Fairy' is massed in large groupings to provide a colorful ground cover at the Antique Rose Emporium in Texas.

The purple gazing ball acts as a mirror reflecting the surrounding scene. 'The Fairy' roses combine with alysum in this small bed.

Specialty Roses

Pegged Roses
Unique Color
Water Feature
Ground Cover
Unique Feature
Cabbage Rose

Pegging Roses

One method of training roses that has been nearly forgotten is called pegging. A rose suitable for pegging will have long flexible canes in the 5-to 7-foot range. A number of Bourbons and Hybrid Perpetuals, as Peter Beales agrees, are "almost custom-built for this purpose." Climbing roses that reach over 7 feet are not good for pegging, as they quickly grow out of bounds and become unattractive .

To peg a rose, fasten the canes to the ground by pinning them with a hook, or "peg". It is important to remember to let new canes harden properly before they are bent down and pegged no matter how unruly they may look; otherwise they may break. We peg our roses twice a year, before the onset of new growth (for us it is late January and late August). We use the long 6-to 7-foot canes that have grown in the prior season. Older canes can be pruned away every second or third year to make room for these newly pegged canes. The canes can be left with a high arch or fastened nearly horizontal, arranged in a perfect wheel around the center of the plant or swirled slightly depending on artistic desire and available space. There are a number of creative ways to use this method, but the end result is basically the same. Pulling the canes horizontally causes the rose to produce flowers at nearly every leaf axil, increasing the blooming potential many fold. A pegged rose is generally used as a specimen plant and takes up quite a bit of space, but the incredible floral display and unique shape make it quite worthwhile to try the technique.

The bouquet (left) shows the beautiful flowers of some Bourbon roses. Bourbon roses resulted from an original cross of 'Autumn Damask' and 'Old Blush' on the Isle of Bourbon, near the coast of Africa. Bourbon roses have qualities from both parents: the hardiness and fragrance of the Damask and the remontancy and the heat tolerance of the Chinas. Bourbons were later bred with other groups of roses like Portlands and Hybrid Chinas which eventually led to new classes like Hybrid Perpetuals and modern Hybrid Teas. Shown are 'Madame Issac Periere', 'Madame Ernest Calvat', 'Souvenir de la Malmaison', and 'Great Western'.

'Madame Ernest Calvat' (above) blooms on pegged canes at the Antique Rose Emporium display garden in San Antonio, Texas. The new growth emerging from the middle of the bush will grow 6 to 7 feet straight up by early fall. These new canes will be pegged just like the existing ones are seen now. They will provide a stunning display of flowers for the fall garden. Some of the older canes that are currently pegged now can be removed to allow room for the new canes.

ROSES SUITED FOR PEGGING

Adam	Mme. Ernest Calvat
Arrillaga	Mme. Isaac Pereire
Frau Karl Druschki	Mme. Plantier
Great Western	Marchioness of
Honorine de Brabrant	Londonderry
Lucetta	Queen of Bourbons
Madame Driout	Variegata di Bologna

Color

Breeders have yet to produce a black rose, or even a true blue rose. With the advent of genetic splicing, created colors in roses are imminent. We have included three naturally bred roses in this section that are sure to create a stir with rose fanciers. Those wanting to add interesting color to their gardening palette need look no further.

Mr. McGregor's farm, a children's garden at the Antique Rose Emporium in Texas, expands the imagination of visitors displaying the bizarre rose by the entryway.

Green Rose, Prior to 1845
R. chinensis viridiflora
China

The 'Green Rose' is Mother Nature's creation. Originally found in China, it has unfortunately suffered from a rash of criticism and damnation by some rosarians. Since its introduction in 1845, 'The Green Rose' was sometimes referred to as *R. monstrosa*. Camouflaged blooms, resembling tufts of leaves, occur spring through fall on a healthy shrub that can grow to 5 feet. Flowers make great additions to arrangements giving contrast to the barrage of bright colors.

Basye's Purple Rose, 1968
Shrub

'Basye's Purple' resulted in the cross between *R. rugosa* and *R. foliosa* . This cross was made by Dr. Robert Basye when he was researching disease resistance in seedlings of wild rose crosses. 'Bayse's Purple' makes an erect bush with prickly canes and rugose foliage. However, its most obvious feature is the flowers. The showy, velvety-purple, single flowers with prominent gold stamens are truly regal. Flowers repeat through the growing season. This rose is extremely cold hardy and thorny.

Smith's Parish
Bermuda Mystery Rose

The island of Bermuda was a hopping off point for travelers from Europe to America, since America's colonization. Roses that survived there had to be tough - withstanding the onslaught of wind, salt spray, and drought. The list of roses that have been rediscovered there is formidable, as chronicled in a book titled, Bermuda Roses written by The Bermuda Rose Society. "Smith's Parish" is an unusual rose of varying color. Large plants to 6 feet taunt the grower with semi-double flowers of white, white with bright red streaks, and deep shades of pink or red. Occasionaly all these color variations will occur on the plant at the same time.

A Rose for a Water Garden

Swamp Rose, Prior to 1824
R. palustras scandens
Species

This rose evolved in America with many specimens happily residing in the sandy, swamp-covered soils of Louisiana and ranging North and eastward to the Carolinas. As an understory plant in forested areas, it has acquired a tolerance to shade as well as heavy, mucky soils.

Architecturally interesting at all times of the year, the 'Swamp Rose' has graceful, arching and nearly thornless branches with narrow, willow like leaves. No plant could be more beautiful-weeping into a stream or reflecting in the water by a pond. Our gardens not only feature it by water's edge, but under the canopy of a large cypress tree. Both situations are anomalies in the traditional use of roses. Flowers are in abundance late in the spring. Redoute painted this rose in the garden of Empress Josephine.

The 'Swamp Rose' is beautiful even when not in flower. Ice covering the cascading branches embellishes its naturally graceful form.

The newly planted water garden (right) looks naked and univiting. In the same garden (below) plants of various sizes and color soften the garden making it much more appealing. The 'Swamp Rose', shown at water's edge nearist the house, is an example of this dramatic transformation.

Ground Cover

Besides providing vertical interest on structures, many climbing roses, if managed properly can provide horizontal service as a ground cover. Ground cover treatments can be tricky with inappropriate site selection and competition from other plants and weeds. Ironically, the best locations are those where no other plants or weeds will grow. Trailing, long-caned roses can be established purposefully in beds or large containers carved out or placed in these areas. Roses throw their expansive canes onto unsightly areas like rock outcrops, steep slopes, and concreted surfaces without the danger of invasive grass and weeds destroying their matted texture covered with flowers.

Red Cascade, 1976
Miniature

'Red Cascade' was introduced in 1976 as a climbing miniature. Prolific canes are very flexible and are covered with small glossy leaves. Plants spread to create a dense, matted ground cover which can then exceed 12 feet in either direction. Small, dark red flowers occur in clusters from April through November with spring and fall flushes being the most dramatic. Its versatility has led us to use her as a climber on a tall pillar, as a ground cover in a rock garden, and in a container where her canes cascade over the edge.

Petite Pink Scotch
Found

   "Petite Pink Scotch" has a habit very different than that of 'Red Cascade'. Tiny leaves cover dozens of arching branches on a shrub 2-foot-tall by 4-foot-wide. The thick, finely textured plants have little resemblance to traditional roses. Blooms are tiny, half inch, pink pompons that tightly cover the canes.

   The rose, found in 1949 by Jackson M. Batchelor of Willard, North Carolina, was growing in the garden of a 1750s plantation home on the Cape Fear River near Wilmington, NC. The area was originally settled by Scottish and English immigrants, and Mr. Batchelor speculates that this rose came with them, explaining the found name given it. (The rose shows no relationship to the 'Scotch Rose', *R. spinosissima*.)   Edging made of rock, wood, or metal around garden beds are accented by "Petite Pink Scotch's" graceful habit.

Chestnut Rose,
Prior to 1814
R. roxburghii
Species

Also known as the "Chinquapin Rose" and "Burr Rose", this is very double, garden form of *R. roxburghii*. The single-flowered form was not found until 1864, growing in China's Szechuan province. William Roxburgh, assistant surgeon to the East India Company, came across this rose in a garden in Canton, China, where it had been grown for generations as 'Hoi-tong-hong'. He sent it to the Calcutta Botanic Garden, from whence it reached England in 1820 and quickly traveled on to America. We find it lingering in many old Southern gardens. The 'Chestnut Rose' is un-ique in many ways. The pink, lightly fragrant flowers open from mossy looking buds irregularly throughout the growing season and are followed by bristly, globular hips that resemble chestnut burrs. The odd, pale brown bark exfoliates like torn paper as the canes gain caliper and the plant gets older. Leaves composed of small leaflets defy an identity as a rose plant. Plants can grow to 8 feet with equal spread.

Thick-foliaged 'Chestnut Roses' provide perfect cover for birds that often nest inside. Dense plants make very effective hedges.

Eglantine,
Prior to 1551

R. eglanteria
Species

This is a favorite English native that has been recorded in literature from Chaucer to Shakespeare as the 'Sweet Brier Rose' because of the strongly apple-scented leaves. *R. eglanteria*, or 'Eglantine', has been common in cottage gardens on both sides of the Atlantic Ocean because it is not only hardy, but always fragrant, whether or not it is in bloom. The rambling shrub is large, thorny, and vigorous with dark green, slightly rough foliage. The spring flowers are single pink with a good rose fragrance of their own. *R. eglanteria* should be part of every fragrance garden; rain, wind and sun all seem to bring out the perfume of the plant. This rose does not sucker and offers an outstanding spring floral display in return for very little care.

Cabbage Rose

Paul Neyron, 1869
Hybrid Perpetual

Imbricated petals in perfect layers emerge from fat magenta rose buds. These rose blooms acquired their name due to the similarity to the impressive vegetable. The original cabbage roses from European descent are *R. centifolia* varieties. Centifolia means one hundred petals. 'Paul Neyron' does not have a hundred petals, but when weather and culture are right, flowers are huge measuring 6-to 7-inches across. This rose wins our approval for its fragrance, hardiness, and repeat bloom, giving it credibility as a good garden plant. A very erect shrub with thornless canes dictate her use as a specimen plant where passersby can marvel at her fragrant giant flowers.

'Paul Neyron's' large pink blooms are obvious in this mixed flower arrangement containing an assortment of roses and perennials. Arrangement by Henry Flowers.

USDA Zone Hardiness Map

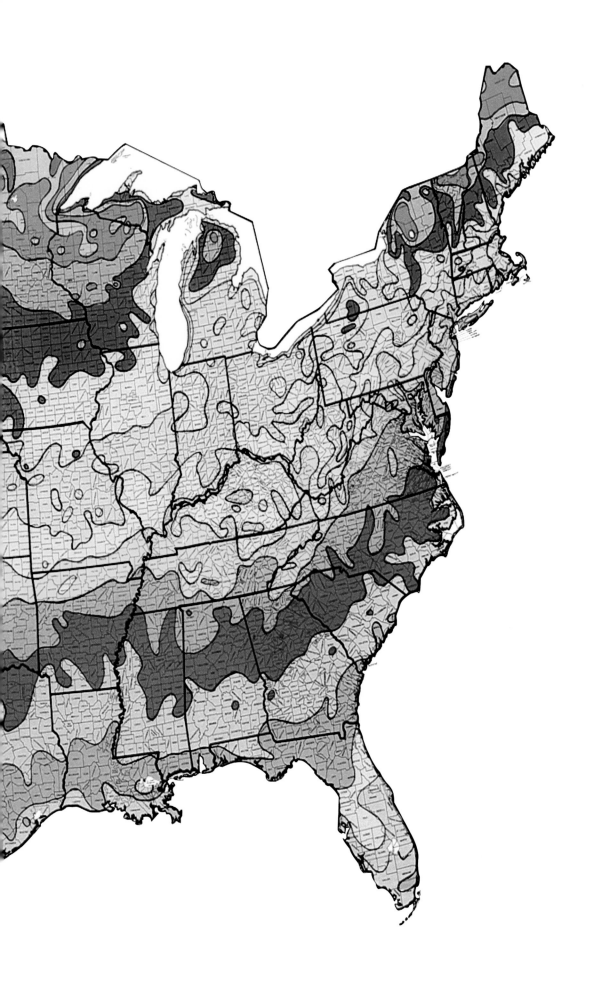

Index